STORMING HOME

"Billy Gilvear is a remarkable man. From a life dominated by family break-up, drugs, and despair, he has been transformed by an encounter with Jesus Christ. He is now a role model for so many people. His story will offer hope to everyone who reads it."
– Revd Nicky Gumbel, Holy Trinity Brompton

"A thriller. The pages of Billy's life seem to turn themselves. All the elements of the greatest adventure story, except this one's true!"
– Revd Anthony Delaney, Leader, Ivy Church, Manchester

"I have seen first-hand just what an incredible impact Billy's testimony has in the prisons and tough communities where we live. I can't wait now to see this amazing story get the wider audience it deserves."
– Andy Hawthorne OBE, CEO of The Message Trust

"From soldier to officer, drug pusher to attempted suicide victim, Billy is an ordinary man who has lived an extraordinary life. No matter how hopeless a situation may appear, his testimony is that there is always hope. I am so glad Billy's remarkable story is now in print, and cannot recommend it highly enough."
– Major Rhett Parkinson RE

"Gritty, punchy, brutally honest, and very real. This is an incredible story of one man's journey through a living hell to redemption. Buy a copy, read it and give it to a mate."
– Carl Beech, General Director, CVM

STORMING HOME

British soldier, Bodyguard to the stars,
Boozer and addict – Could Billy change?

BILLY GILVEAR
AND ERIC GAUDION

MONARCH
BOOKS

Oxford, UK & Grand Rapids, Michigan, USA

Published by Monarch Books
an imprint of
Lion Hudson plc
Wilkinson House, Jordan Hill Road,
Oxford OX2 8DR, England
Email: monarch@lionhudson.com
www.lionhudson.com/monarch

ISBN 978 0 85721 255 9
e-ISBN 978 0 85721 460 7

First edition 2013

Acknowledgments
Unless otherwise stated, Scripture quotations are taken from the Holy
Bible, New International Version Anglicised. Copyright © 1979, 1984,
2011 Biblica, formerly International Bible Society. Used by permission
of Hodder & Stoughton Ltd, an Hachette UK company. All rights
reserved. "NIV" is a registered trademark of Biblica. UK trademark
number 1448790.
Other Scripture taken from the New King James Version®. Copyright
© 1982 by Thomas Nelson, Inc. Used by permission. All rights
reserved.

A catalogue record for this book is available from the British Library

Printed and bound in the UK, May 2013, LH26

To my beautiful wife, Bev –

Without you there would be no book, for without you there would be no story of transformation. The love and commitment you have shown have kept me alive. On those occasions when I wanted to give up, feeling worthless and empty, you stood by me, speaking words of love and affirmation over me. Where others saw destruction, you saw hope; where others saw death, you saw life. You are the greatest woman I know, and I thank God every day for you.

Contents

Acknowledgments

To all my family especially Mum, Dad, Catriona, and Judith, for the love, prayers, and patience you have shown. Thank you: I love you more than words can express.

To my children, Jordan, Jack, Ben, and Lydia: thank you for the inspiration you have given me to keep going when so many times I wanted to give up. I hope in life you practise all that you have inspired in me and no matter what life throws at you, never give up! I love you loads x

To all my friends who have been part of this story (you know who you are), for the love shown and support given, thank you so much; without you I would never have made it.

To Eric, thank you for the time and effort you have taken over our project. For the opportunities you have now given me and for simply not giving up on me, thank you.

Billy Gilvear

FOREWORD

I heartily recommend this account of Billy Gilvear's life and his remarkable transformation to you. I do so for at least three reasons.

First, this is an *authentic* account. It is authentic in every way. For one thing, it is a true account: I know Billy and count it a privilege to be his friend, and I also know those who have known him since before he came to faith. This really happened. For another, it is also authentic because it is about the real world. Indeed, much of it is about a dark, troubled, and painful world, so nasty that we might well wish that it was not real. It is authentic in another way too: Billy has made no attempt to varnish over what he once was and the real struggles he had in breaking free from his past.

Second, this is an *extraordinary* account. This is not a story of a slightly bad person becoming a slightly good person. On the contrary: this is the story of a very bad person being so utterly changed that he now delights in being a child of God. It is the story of someone who was utterly without hope becoming someone who shares hope with others. Billy, once the sort of person that you would have been very wise to cross the street to avoid, is now a gentleman who is a joy to be with. This is an astounding, night-to-day, despair-to-joy, total turnaround that would be utterly unbelievable except for the fact that it happens to be true.

Third, this is an *encouraging* account. There is encouragement here *to pray*. There seems little doubt that behind the extraordinary events detailed in this book lie the fervent prayers of Billy's long-suffering parents. What we read here should encourage us to pray – and to continue to pray – for those whom God has put on our hearts. There is encouragement here, too, *to preach*. The proclamation of the good news of Jesus arouses opposition and it's easy to let it slip off the agenda. Yet what we read here reminds us that the gospel – and only the gospel – truly transforms lives. Above all, there is encouragement *to believe*. If you have not yet put your faith in Jesus Christ, then read this book and begin your journey of faith. You may protest that you are too bad for God to do anything with, but this book brings you the best of news – if Jesus can redeem a man like Billy Gilvear then he can redeem you.

Reverend Canon J. John
www.philotrust.com

I

"D" (FOR DARKEST) DAY

This would be it, then – 20 December 2000 – "D" Day, for the darkest day of my wretched life.

The fact that it was my birthday made it seem even more appropriate to plan to go ahead on that day, a kind of poetic justice. I had everything ready. After the mess I had made last time I tried this, I was determined to make a really good job of it. There was this guy on the TV news who had topped himself by looking on one of the sites on the Internet that tell people how to kill themselves. What a weirdo! But now I found myself drawn to his web pages like a fly to an ultraviolet electric death trap. I had done my research well and I was all set for the off. I planned to kill myself on that day. I had just over two weeks to live.

I had begun my research in the same way as the geek I had seen on the Net. The next time someone was going into Newport and could give me a lift, I jumped at the chance.

Once there I made my way to the public library, where I knew I could use one of the computers set aside for people doing research. I was amazed by how easy it was to find this kind of material online. Even at the time I was looking, a good many years ago, the Internet was already huge. The following year the latest academic estimate from the US was that the Web had some 800 million pages, but today that number exceeds 9 billion pages and is rising steadily.[1] True, there were some sites that aimed to help people who were considering suicide by trying to dissuade them, but I wasn't interested in those. Looking more deeply into the darker side of the World Wide Web, I searched for the most common ways of doing away with oneself, and the most effective. I decided that I was going to hang myself, as that seemed to be the favoured method of the day. I researched the noose that would do the job well, and noted the tips for a so-called "successful outcome". As soon as I got back to the farm I would start looking for a quiet place where I could do what I had to do, in the knowledge that nobody would find me, not in time at any rate.

In those days I was really just wandering around in a stupor. It was probably the loneliest time of my life. I used to wake up early in the mornings really fed up that I had not died in my sleep. I felt wretched, washed up, a waste of space. I would think of my ex-wife, Bev, and my sons, Jordan and Jack, who were living just a few miles away, and it all seemed so utterly hopeless. My parents would be broken-hearted when they heard – but, hey, I broke their hearts years ago, so they had had plenty of time to practise. Anyway, they are Christians, retired missionaries from the African Congo, so are they not supposed to forgive? I knew that I had messed up completely and felt that I was good for nothing now. I was like the walking dead – like a prisoner on death row, just waiting for my date with destiny. Emotionally I felt that I was stinging all over, yet strangely inert at the deepest level. My

---

1   http://www.worldwidewebsize.com

heart burned so much that it was physically painful. It seemed as if my whole body was on fire with the raging agony of my foolishness, and at that moment I could see no other way out. My desolation was complete.

Then, one day when I was out working with the other lads, I found what I thought would be the perfect spot. We had a big slurry tank that from time to time needed to be cleaned out. It stood about 5 metres high and was like a huge metal cylinder painted green. We were sent there to do the job, and we used the ladder that was fixed to the side to get us up into the top part to clean it out properly.

It was while I was up there that I saw my ideal place. Near the top of the ladder and high up inside the open rim of the bin I saw that there were some strong metal hooks set into the steel. I had no idea what they were for, but I tested them out while I was fiddling around up there and decided that here was where my useless life would end. I reached out and tugged on one again just to see if it would hold my weight, which wasn't much in those days anyway. It held fast and seemed just right. Once the cleaning team was well out of the place the bin would lie idle for a few weeks until a whole load of cow manure from the nearby yard and slurry pit would be pumped into it. This would give me plenty of time to do the deed. It held one hundred thousand gallons (454,600 litres) of animal manure, and that's what my life had become, addled by alcohol, drugs, and outbursts of rage from my vile temper. I was utterly alone. It seemed like poetic justice to end my useless days in a place built to hold muck.

Little did I know that, by the time that day finally came, I would be hanging my life on something else completely. When that dismal dawn broke my attitude had actually turned upside down – or maybe right side up – and I had turned my filthy life over to the power of Jesus Christ to forgive and make me clean. In spite of all my careful plans for total self-destruction, I was unprepared for the tsunami that was about to overflow my stubborn defences. If you had told me that then, I would have laughed in your face – or spat in it!

2

ROOTS AND SHOOTS

You never would have thought my life was going to turn out this way. My parents were full-time evangelical Christian workers serving in the former Belgian Congo and afterwards in the UK in various mission-related capacities. Bill Gilvear, my dad, is a very well-known and highly respected figure in certain church circles, mainly the Brethren or Free Evangelicals.

Mum and Dad told me that when I was born, in Kisangani in a remote area of the Congo, they thought that their firstborn would die almost immediately. An amazing series of coincidences had led up to my birth and made my parents aware that God was involved in my arrival on earth, but the whole thing was touch and go. I entered the world fighting to survive, and I suppose that struggle has continued ever since. My mum was desperately ill with a cyst in the womb during her pregnancy and they lived in a remote and hostile place. An operation was needed to save my mum's life, but the missionary doctor on that remote Congo station presumed that there was no way that I could be saved. The unborn baby would have to be sacrificed to save its mother. My mum told me that she was in despair at being in that faraway, alien location and asked herself why she couldn't have been at home near the Queen Mother's Hospital in Glasgow instead of stuck out in the African jungle.

In desperation, and anxious not to abandon a pregnancy for which they had waited so long and prayed so much, they both got down on their knees and begged God to help them. After that my dad had a brainwave and made contact by radio with a specialist gynaecologist working in the Congo. She was located five days' journey away overland, and there was no way my heavily pregnant mother could make that trip. On air the lady doctor said that she could perform the operation and still keep me, the baby, intact in my mother's womb, but it just seemed impossible to get her into that operating theatre.

Apparently, it was amazing how each overwhelming difficulty was overcome. Without delay, and in the face of all kinds of problems, a plane came down from the far-off mission station and whisked Mum away. Dad told me that there was a rule that the tiny Mission Aviation Fellowship aircraft were allowed to land on government-owned airstrips only during public holidays, but as the next day was to be such a holiday, he and Mum were flown out then, just in time.

The surgery was delicate and dangerous but many folk were praying, and it was successful. Immediately following the operation, however, my poor mother caught malaria, and once again it was amazing that the pregnancy remained intact.

Yet the story of the miracles surrounding my birth did not end there. Further problems occurred when it was found that this tiny baby was Rhesus positive, the opposite of my mum. A rare vaccine would need to be administered straight away to overcome this potentially deadly complication. There was just none of this anti-Rhesus globulin anywhere in the Congo or thereabouts in Africa, but my mum told me that, just when they were giving up hope, some was found in the laboratory of a chemical factory in Dublin, thousands of kilometres away in Ireland. "Billy", she used to say to me, "it was a wonderful answer to prayer how that vaccine reached us in the jungle." I would grin and just shrug my shoulders when I was old enough to understand, but it did seem strange to me how, by a series of seemingly chance encounters with missionaries at Heathrow Airport and in the capital of the Congo, Kinshasa, the vaccine was finally delivered to my cot side.

So I was meant to be born alive, but, by the time of my repeated suicide attempts in Wales, I had forgotten that completely.

✳✳✳✳

I was less than a year old when the family moved from Africa back to Scotland. We lived with my mum's parents when we first got there. Mum and Dad desperately needed accommodation of a more permanent kind following a serious injury to my dad's arm that required urgent surgical treatment. Driving on the harsh African roads had taken its toll and put enormous pressure on an old injury. "Sure, it's like driving over a scrubbing board like my old Mammy used to take to the Steamie," he would say, making light of the agony he was in. Eventually it became clear to my parents that they needed to return to the UK for Dad to get the help he needed. Unsure of how to find a place to stay, Dad attended a service in what was their sending church – the Tent Hall in Glasgow. Amazingly, the speaker turned out to be a "Glasgow house factor" with access to properties around the city, and, as a result of his meeting my dad that day, we were offered a tiny two-room apartment with kitchen in Elderslie Street.

This accommodation was part of a tenement block near Glasgow city centre. We had to climb two flights of stairs, something that my mum tells me was a real trial for her with my pram and the shopping, especially as Dad's arm was by then in heavy plaster so he couldn't help her. The tiny kitchen had a cooker that was often hidden from view by a line of washing hanging limp across the room like bunting in the rain.

I can still smell the tantalizing aroma of Mum's cooking in that kitchen. She would do the washing on a Saturday, when she would also bake truly mouth-watering cakes and bread. Even the dried washing retained smells that made my mouth water so that I loved putting a clean vest over my head and taking time to inhale the aroma. At first it was just my parents and me in the little flat until my sister Catriona came along when I was two.

It was quite a tense period, because when our little family group came back from Africa we had no money. As a result it was a miracle that we got Elderslie Street. My parents worked for the Unevangelised Fields Mission, part of what was known as the faith movement. One of its tenets was that no missionary or worker should speak about money or make their needs known to anyone except to God in prayer. They believed that God would supply everything in that way and that meant salary, house, and all else besides. Looking back, it was quite phenomenal, because God always *did* supply their needs, and they would refuse to take charity because they just believed God would provide everything.

After Elderslie Street we moved to a part of Glasgow called Arden. It was a major post-war housing development, consisting, like a typical Glasgow estate, of high flats and tenements. After setting up home twice in a short time we had no money left. My dad felt this lack of funds keenly and it forced him to try to do something about it, despite his principles. I remember going with him and some other child to the Social Security office, where he would ask for help. He used to get really angry because we had so little. It certainly wasn't easy for my parents when we first came back from the Congo.

Much later, my dad, who was still a missionary even though we were back in the UK, got a job with the Royal Sailors' Rests (RSR) in Helensburgh. This small country town stands on the banks of the River Clyde, close to the beautiful countryside of Loch Lomond and the Trossachs National Park, where the West Highlands meet the Lowlands. RSR, often known as "Aggies", is a Christian charity that provides "people, places, and projects" in support of the Royal Navy. In existence for the last 130 years, RSR gives support to the Royal Naval Chaplaincy Service by means of on-base pastoral workers at many Royal Navy and Royal Marines establishments. My dad became one of those "Missioners", as they were called, and we moved to a large house known as Gully Bridge. It was designed to provide a Christian, alcohol-free, family leisure centre for serving personnel and their families, situated close to the Royal Naval Port area at Helensburgh. That became our first real home and was near my first school, Rhu Primary. On the day that Mum and Dad moved to it I had been scheduled to have my adenoids removed in hospital. My poor mum didn't know which way to turn because she wanted to be with me on the ward and yet she also felt obliged to help her family move to their new home. In the end Mum's parents – my grandparents – came to visit me on the hospital ward for the limited hour or so each day that was allowed at that time while she oversaw the move.

I have really good memories of living in Helensburgh. The house itself was huge and felt like a mansion to me. The time in Glasgow had been hard and discouraging for us all. I remember Dad, in particular, being really weighed down by a heavy sense of frustration and anger. But once we moved to Helensburgh things started looking up at first. Little did I know then, though, how hard life was to become for me, but at that early stage I recall a real sense of relief sweeping over me that our situation might be improving after all. It was a centre for sailors who were serving on submarines to come and have a break during their time ashore, in a relaxing atmosphere that was fundamentally free of alcohol.

Actually I was quite free there, because it is such a rambling old house with many rooms, staircases, and places for a growing boy to play and to hide in. We had our own private living quarters upstairs. The centre was surrounded by huge grounds. We had a boat, canoes, scuba diving kits, and all manner of interesting things to see and do. The guys could come and use all that. We even had airguns. They used to set up an airgun range and I think they killed a few rabbits too. All this provided great excitement for a growing boy, and my fondest childhood memories were formed in that house. Sailors would come and play football with me, or tennis – all the sorts of things a father and son might have done in other circumstances. But Dad was too busy or just too preoccupied to give me that kind of attention, and the lack of communication between us began to grow and fester.

Life in Helensburgh began to revolve around people staying at the centre, who included me in their sport and recreation. Summers were great, with the smell of the newly mown lawns around the place combining with that of the freshly baked bread from my mum's kitchen. Mum would sometimes stand beside the badminton court on the lawn and watch as we played against the sailors or some visiting missionary. There were a lot of missionaries who would stay with us while they were visiting churches around the area on furlough: the huge house had space for them all. Sometimes I found these people strange. They seemed old-fashioned in their manner of dress and quite severe too in the way they behaved. I was often reminded that "children are meant to be seen and not heard", and I developed a knack of keeping clear of them as often as I could, preferring the company of the service personnel from the base.

Unfortunately, there were also some very difficult times for me in Helensburgh, as it was there that my dad's frustration and temper got the better of him on occasion. My dad has a tremendous story of his own upbringing and survival through the horrors of the wild areas of old Glasgow and the gang warfare into which he was thrust at an early age. As a child he was physically abused in the east end of Glasgow, where he lived with his brothers and sisters and his parents. When my grandfather died my grandmother took in a lodger to help cope with the expenses the family was facing. My father was the eldest but he was beaten regularly by the lodger. In those days they didn't have ChildLine for an abuse victim to call, or any counselling, and they certainly didn't talk about feelings.

I suppose he just bottled it all up, but inevitably the pain and horror that my father had been through had to come out, and unfortunately it definitely affected our relationship. I know that once we returned from Africa – after his surgery he was unable to go back to the Congo – he was a very unhappy and at times unwell man. The atmosphere of tension in our home, and the accompanying fear, made me start to think negatively about the claims of Christianity and the God of love whom believers spoke about yet who seemed strangely absent from my dad's dealings with me.

I realize now that Dad was very much a product of his own era and, of course, he never knew the joy of a father's love himself. I also think that what really motivated quite a few Christians back then was the fear of the Lord rather than his grace. I was always scared of God, just as everyone seemed to be, but I was *really* scared of my dad. It seemed to me then that Christianity was all about being afraid of God's wrath and of hellfire, and there was very little mention of his grace.

I knew that my dad was totally committed to the church and to his ministry, but I didn't get much time with him. Despite the unhappy times we experienced I longed for his attention and for his affirmation of me as his son. We just didn't get the kind of "father and son" time that you would normally expect. There was a complete breakdown in our communication and the result for me was a sense of real loss that I would carry with me for the rest of my life. It made me realize the true importance and significance of the love of a father.

In the midst of some difficult times at home, my mother worked tirelessly to bring about peace. Her love for me then was all-encompassing and total, as it still is now. I remember sitting on her lap as she used to read books to me and my sister Catriona with great passion, making every syllable come alive for us and every sentence a feast of the imagination. In the evenings she would sit by my bed and comfort me when things were hard, encouraging me to really go for it in life. I also remember Christmases in our house being the most amazing times, mostly thanks to Mum, who would always pull out all the stops. She was and still is the most remarkable woman.

There was also a surprise addition to our family when another sister came along. Judith arrived when I was fourteen, and when I returned home each morning after doing my milk round I would make her porridge for breakfast, allowing Mum to have a lie-in.

I am very proud of both my sisters and all that they have achieved in their own lives. Catriona went on to become a Detective Chief Inspector with the Central Scotland Police and Judith has grown into a fine sportswoman, co-ordinating sports education for her local schools. They are both loving mothers as well now, but as brother and sisters we are very close. Eventually I would go on to learn through them and my mother what God's love really looks like, but for a long time – three decades, in fact – I couldn't see the wood for the trees.

Later in life I looked back at my dad's story and came to appreciate how horrific his childhood was. He was ill treated and beaten by alcoholic lodgers, and as you read his terrible story in the book about his life, *Rough Diamond*,[2] you can just imagine the extreme and dark places where Dad was taken as a child.

He too was the eldest of the family and felt the responsibility keenly, and he must have felt so frustrated as he witnessed his poor mum constantly being beaten up while he could do so little to prevent it. Life was violent in general, and when it came to the discipline of children, especially sons, the culture of Glasgow's tenements presumed that you take your punishment like a man, and it was invariably brutal. It was also still in the age of capital punishment, and a couple of Dad's gangs' colleagues and close friends were hanged in HM Prison Barlinnie for committing murder.

---

2   *Rough Diamond: The Life Story of Bill Gilvear*, Sheena Brown (Christian Focus Publications, Fearn, Ross-shire, 1996).

I was the first male contact he had had in a family context since all that, and he thought that this brutality was just what you did. This was the era he was living in, and from which the newly minted Christian Bill Gilvear came. He had an amazing transformation when he found Christ as his saviour, but, as with all of us, his upbringing was still there and it affected him at times of stress especially, such as occurred following his return from Africa and during the breakdowns that he endured. I understand this now because I have suffered in times of stress too. In my case it was when I was working as a prison chaplain and was involved in the care of offenders at high risk of committing suicide, and of their families in the aftermath. I found myself reverting to unhelpful and unhealthy patterns of thought and even behaviour. God had mercy on me and helped me through those dark periods and so I feel a sense of understanding now, but at that early stage none of this made any sense to my mind at all.

By the time I moved to secondary school home life was taking its toll on me emotionally. I was also really cynical about the faith that I had been brought up to profess. I still did not have a voice but I was starting to have opinions, and I knew it would not be long before my views started to clash very badly with those of my father.

You might wonder whether I tried to speak up for myself as I got older, and to a certain extent I tried and failed. In the end I just withdrew inside myself. I made sure that I kept away from Dad. I just didn't talk to him any more and we seldom, if ever, communicated. He would try sometimes, telling me that "No one is against you, Billy" or similar phrases, but it was always very awkward, forced, and artificial.

I withdrew from my family and became a real dreamer. At first they were dreams of escaping. My parents and teachers used to say that my head was "full of wee doors and they're all chapping", an old Scottish saying, and they were right. I'm still quite a dreamer, but at that time reality seemed just too scary for me to think about so my dream world became my alternative reality. When people said of me, "He's a dreamer", I would think, "Too right I am", because dreaming was my freedom card. I used to dream at school and all the way home, and especially when I was at home.

I would go to my room in the evenings instead of sitting downstairs, because I liked being in there when the lights were off. I would put on my little clock radio and listen to it. Tiger Tim was on Radio Clyde then and I would listen to some music and quietly drift away to my dream land where I felt safe. I dreamed of places that were quiet, peaceful, and devoid of fear and upset, such as distant holiday islands with sandy beaches kissed by constant sun and clear blue sea.

That dream existence, which allowed me to avoid distress and painful thoughts, became a way of life right up to my time in the army, when I started to face some of my early fears. Then the emotional pain of all the rejection and loneliness that I had experienced began to come back, and it affected me quite negatively. That was probably about two years into the army. I sought escape from mental pain in any way that I could, and I think that the sensations produced by alcohol became something that could finally take me away and let me escape from my bewilderment. You see, by then I was really confused about life. I just thought, "What is this all about?" Once again the familiar refrain haunted me: "You tell me 'You need Jesus, you need God', but, hang on, *you're* the guy that I need and you are just not there for me!" It became very confusing. Alcohol, and then later the drugs and medications that I abused, offered a means of escape from all this mental turmoil.

I am not trying to make excuses for all the bad choices that I would later make, but I do think that the roots of my many failures in life were buried in this confusion, and would surface to trip me up with almost fatal consequences. My feet were on a very slippery slope from an early age.

Back then, though, in my early teens, I wanted to live out my dreams and find utopia. I know that I didn't look for it in the right place, which would have been in Jesus, but I was always trying to find something that could take the pain away. I didn't want to face myself because I felt that my past had damaged my thinking and affected my head completely. Since then, of course, I've been through counselling, which has helped me a great deal, and in due time I needed to sit down and talk all of this through with my elderly dad, and that was very hard to do. I have also discovered that even as a Christian you still face issues that arise from your inner self and the past. I have made wrong choices too as an adult and a Christian leader, and have had to repent and change my thinking on a daily basis.

Things are better between my dad and me now, and I understand more of the struggles that he was dealing with from his own past, but I feel sad that we'll never have the relationship that we should have had – it just cannot be. There is still a sense of sadness in my heart about a lost relationship in childhood. Like water held in the hand, it is so hard to get back what you have lost. Thankfully I have found a God who promises to do just that in our lives, but at that early stage I would have laughed at that idea.

In my adolescent agony of mind I often wanted to die because I felt worthless, and that low sense of self-worth has pursued me over the years like an angry bull into whose field I had strayed. I also think that's why I looked for approval from sergeant majors, officers, and then the stars for whom I did close protection work. That is part of the reason why I did so well in the army and the protection business. I was really committed and quite determined, but I was looking for something; I wanted the approval of a father figure. I was longing for some person in authority to say, "Well done, my son". But, of course, they rarely could and they very seldom did, not to my satisfaction at least.

The voice I really wanted to hear remained silent.

3

ESCAPE TO THE ARMY

I had first applied to join the army when I was legally allowed to do so, at fifteen and a half. Actually, I went to the Army Careers Office when I was fourteen and they told me to come back in a year's time. I was so keen to leave home that it seemed like an age till I would be old enough. The atmosphere at home was really tense by then.

Looking back now I can see what a typically awkward teenager I was, but there was much more than that pushing me towards the armed forces. At the tender age of fifteen I thought I was a man. After all the arguments and bust-ups I'd had with Dad, running off to join the army was very much an escape route. It offered me the hope of safety too: somewhere I could run away to hide but have a roof over my head and three meals a day, and where nobody could force me to go back home. I reckoned that in that environment I'd be appreciated and valued, and learn something new – maybe see the world, as the advert said, and have a life of adventure.

Also, joining the army suited my kind of personality, which was quite driven and sporty, and dreaming of adventure. During those years of playing sport and having fun with the guys from the Royal Navy base in Scotland I had developed a real fantasy about the wonderful life of adventure and comradeship that awaited me in the armed forces. The sailors would regale this eager young lad with tales of faraway places and hair-raising adventures, and it all seemed so alluring. And of course it also suited my need to get out of my home.

We were living in Denny then, a town of just under ten thousand people in the Falkirk area of Scotland. As soon as I was old enough, I went through to Glasgow by bus on my own and made my way to the Army Careers Office.

What a shock awaited me there. The office itself was fairly Spartan. The only real colour was in the window display, which featured the Union flag and vivid pictures of men in action, but once you entered the door the decor was all boringly brown and cream, with a few rather dreary posters on a small noticeboard. My nose twitched at the acrid smell of disinfectant, and the floor was covered in brown lino just like we'd had in the hallway at Aggie Weston's in Gully Bridge.

That, however, was the only thing there that was in any way reminiscent of home. In fact, those of us who had come to join up were crammed onto two hard wooden benches that lined the walls to the left and the right of the door. They faced the only desk, which was a bare dark wooden table with a pile of forms stacked in the middle. As I made my way gingerly through the door and found a place on the left-hand bench, I began to realize straight away that, compared with the others, I was so very young. I was the most junior person present by far, as everyone else there was joining as an adult. The Junior Leaders Regiment recruited in the normal way at that time, so we were all in together.

I walked into that recruiting centre as a little boy and faced the enormous sergeant major who was standing behind the desk, resplendent in full uniform. He looked terrifying and glared down at me as I hoisted myself up onto the bench, causing my feet to swing a few inches above the ground. After sitting there for a while my bottom had begun to hurt and I squirmed with discomfort, hoping this would not take too long. His face darkened.

"Name?" he bellowed, as if he was on the parade ground at Buckingham Palace, while fixing me with an unblinking stare.

"Gilvear, sir, William," I stammered in response. My voice had not yet quite broken so it came out in a high-pitched whisper that caused a giggle to run up the bench beside me as if I had tickled them all.

"Address?" and so the interrogation went on, as sweat broke out on my brow.

All the guys around me in the waiting area had tattoos on various parts of their body and looked like heavy drinkers and smokers, which really worried me then, but I expected not to be with them for long. Wrong! All those who wanted to join up, including little me, were told that we had to do the selection weekend at Redford Barracks in Edinburgh together. I thought the others had probably already started their careers in life before this foray into the forces. Maybe they were joiners or plumbers or bricklayers, for, as I sat in my place in the queue, they looked quite old to me. "Goodness me, I'm like their younger brother here," I thought nervously, as I pushed out my chest in a vain attempt to make myself look manlier. Some of them were smoking and the fumes produced by the cheap tobacco made my eyes water. After the interviews they were saying to each other and to us all, "Later we'll all go down to the pub and have a pint, eh?"

I'd never been in a pub before, partly because of my tender age but also on account of my parents' strict evangelical upbringing, so it dawned on me that I was entering into a man's world regardless of my age. I also realized that if I was going to join in with these people I was going to have to grow up pretty quickly. My friends back home in Denny, at least those who were still at school, were doing the equivalent of GCSEs and were going to the youth club to play table tennis and enjoy soft drinks. Here I was with these hairy, scary guys who were in their late twenties, and some even in their early thirties, who wanted to take me out to the pub! It was a real wake-up call for me, and I had not even been accepted into the army yet.

My parents didn't know what I was up to, although they probably had an inkling of what was to come. When I got home and told my mum and dad that I had joined the army, they were really mad. I just stood my ground and said, "Look, here's the paperwork. You'll have to sign it." My mum in particular was devastated, but I went to work on her because I needed their signed consent. She was the one who completed the parental approval papers first. She took her time over them and she was really upset that she had to do it, but in the end she realized that she couldn't stop me because I was determined, and if she didn't sign I'd find another way. So in the end she signed, very reluctantly. My dad was absolutely appalled too. I was prepared for that and had just made up my mind that I was not going to let him stop me from getting away.

I found out that I had been accepted into the Junior Leaders section of the army in November 1986, just before my sixteenth birthday, which was on 20 December. So I had my last Christmas at home that year. It was quite a sad time for all my family, I think, and then, on 6 January 1987, Dad took me to the bus.

4

FREEDOM AT LAST?

Leaving day dawned full of hope for me as well as nervousness. I was slightly worried that I might not like the army, or be able to cope with the discipline or the training, but I was determined to go ahead. It was quiet at breakfast, but not so much because of tension, I think, as from sadness on my parents' part. Dad coughed occasionally and Mum made small weeping sounds in between fetching bowls of steaming porridge and pouring tea.

I think Dad regretted not having a close relationship with his son. In fact, after I left home, my sister told me that he spiralled into a state of abject despair and decline. She told me that he would cry and get very upset and depressed, because of course we had missed the opportunity to have the kind of relationship that fathers and sons are meant to have. But, on the day itself, he steeled himself to insist that we bow our heads to say a prayer as I stood trembling in the front room, my knuckles white with tension on the handle of my case. Then he prayed for me and held out a copy of the Bible, which he said I should take with me, but I didn't want to accept it. I shook my head fiercely and averted my eyes. It was a real stand-off and I was frightened. This was a big moment for him as well, and we both knew it. I was thinking, "How can you give me this Bible when you know that I don't believe in God?" I didn't say those words out loud but that's what was going through my mind. I was angry, but I was also afraid, even then, especially on that day. I was still in fear of him and what he might do, even perhaps that he might withdraw consent for me to enlist.

I pushed away my father's precious Bible and waited with trepidation to see what his reaction would be. His eyes began to water a bit, and he looked down at the floor. He was sad. He didn't do what he normally would have done and get angry or yell at me. He just looked a bit lost. Afterwards, when I was reflecting on it all, I felt sorry for him. If I'm honest, there was also emotional turmoil in me. After all, he *was* my dad, and I loved him, but that feeling wouldn't last long. Even the walk down to the bus stop was undertaken in a kind of embarrassing silence, with each of us staring straight ahead. Cars rushed past us causing us to wince in the powerful blast of their slipstream, the angry noise of their straining engines and hot tyres making speech impossible anyway. It was a very difficult day. As I look back on it now I realize it must have been very painful for him, but he put me on that bus to Glasgow with my case. Once there, I joined the rest of the recruits and we caught the train down to Harrogate.

As I sat on that bus in Denny ready to set off for my new life in the army, I was full of mixed emotions. On one level I tingled with real excitement, but I was genuinely moved by the sight of my father's face. I felt such sadness looking back at him from the window of the bus. It was a bitterly cold day and the glass was already steaming up, so I wiped the heavy moisture with the back of my hand, hearing the squeak of the greasy pane and smelling the metallic tang on my wet skin. A metre or so below in the swirling diesel exhaust fumes he looked up at me so crestfallen, sad, and confused. Then the bus shuddered as the main door was slammed shut and, with a throaty roar from the massive engine, we were pulling away, my dad seemingly trying to run alongside for a few metres as if he could prolong our actual parting.

The sight of him moved me very deeply and there was quite a lump in my throat, but almost as soon as the bus rounded the first bend several minutes later it was as if that just didn't matter any more. It may just have been a bend in the road to Glasgow, but for me it was a massive turning of the corner in my life.

In Glasgow we were met by the towering sergeant major from the Army Careers Office. All the recruits that day were destined for the Junior Leaders and so we were all sixteen years old. When we boarded the train we were fizzing and bursting like bottles of pop with excitement, anticipation, and fear. By that stage my family was forgotten. Maybe many who join the army at that tender age have something back home that they want to forget or escape. Perhaps that is what motivates them to give up what should be a loving, supportive family network and leave it for an extreme kind of life. In hindsight, there were probably more sad stories on that train than I realized, but on the day we were so mesmerized and distracted by the new sights and smells of our journey that we couldn't have cared less about each other's worries. There was also a good deal of jostling for status going on, as is often the case with groups of new recruits in any profession, and we desperately wanted to impress the others with our strength and bravado.

Fourteen of us were travelling by rail to join up that day. At the time you could still smoke on the train. Now ordinarily I didn't smoke, but I did that day, just because I could. The beer was flowing too, the smell of it cloying our clothes and spilling over onto anything we touched or bumped into, and there was quite a lot of that going on! I'd come of age now, and Dad wasn't there any more. This was liberation! By the time we got to York we were well on our way to getting drunk. This was my very first encounter with intoxicating drink so it didn't take much for me to get plastered. Once in York Station we piled out of the train to get some more beer.

By the time we got to Harrogate there were fourteen very drunk and rowdy Scotsmen on that train, and complaints had gone ahead of us to the army camp. We were met at the station by two surly and burly NCOs, who frogmarched us over to a waiting green, 3-tonne Bedford lorry, the back of which was covered with heavy-duty green canvas. We had to wait while a couple of the lads were busy being sick on the road. This really angered the NCOs, who yelled at them intimidatingly, urging them to get on board.

Then we piled into the back, struggling to climb over the seemingly mountainous tailgate with all our kit in a state of drunken giggles and helpless falling about. As the lorry lurched and jerked through the town and on to the camp, lads were hanging their heads over the tailgate and holding up the canvas screen, desperate to get some air.

Once through the barracks gates we were lined up in front of the HQ building, totally incapable. They kept us there for what seemed like ages, until finally the most imposing character stepped slowly towards us, glaring like an angry bull about to charge. It turned out that this uniformed behemoth was the commanding officer, who had come out of his office to blast us for letting down our country and letting down the law, the uniform, the regiment, and ourselves.

It was as we were receiving that well-deserved bawling-out that it dawned on me that we had actually arrived and that we were now in the British Army. The party had ended and we were being made aware that it was going to be very serious from here on in. We were screamed at and sworn at and we didn't get any kind of welcome. We watched other recruits being received quite pleasantly, but the Scottish group were in real trouble from the off. We were run ragged and told to "pick up your cases and get over there, you shower of so-and-so's!" Later on I sat on my suitcase and said to myself, "Wow – the honeymoon really is over!" It was quite a wake-up call.

The barracks at Harrogate were known as the Army College. This contained the Junior Leader regiments and also trade schools, mainly for the signals regiments. There were apprentices from Harrogate alongside us in the Junior Leaders. We were training to be infantry and there was great rivalry between the two outfits. I remember walking into our quarters that first day and looking at the floor in the barrack block: I had never seen such a shiny floor in all my life. The old lino was so highly polished you could see your face in it! The pungent smell of polish and disinfectant filled the air and not a mark was visible. Then we were allocated our beds and I discovered that mine was in a side room with four bedsteads lined up in each of two rows, so I realized that I was going to share a room with seven other recruits. This was the first time in my life that I had slept in a room with so many strangers. I soon discovered that we did everything in public. Even the showers were communal, and the toilets had no doors on them. Privacy was at an end for me, and it was quite a shock.

There were forty-eight recruits altogether in my intake, from all different parts of the UK. Quite quickly I began to make friends with one or two, realizing that I would need allies if I was going to survive. One of those early contacts was Neil Pollitt, who had come all the way from Kenya, where he had been at boarding school. His father worked in the banks of Mombasa so he came from a very wealthy family. Neil became a very close friend of mine. Another fellow who remains the best of mates with me even now was called Dave Pilling. He was a big karate fan who pinned up pictures of Bruce Lee on his wall once we were allowed to have posters of our own. I had no idea then, of course, that he would go on to be best man at my wedding several years later.

Within two hours of our inauspicious arrival we were introduced to our room NCOs – and they weren't very nice at all! They just shouted and screamed at us continually. They were Junior Leaders themselves who had been promoted, and they were brutal. Thankfully we found that there would also be some adults in charge of our training, who were senior NCOs. Our platoon sergeant, Roy Partington, had done many years in the army before being appointed a senior instructor for the Royal Signals. His Liverpool accent revealed him as a real "Scouser" with a heart of gold. He had been brought up on the Protestant side of that somewhat divided community. When Church Parade came along on Sundays he would yell out, "Now, all you fine Protestant boys, line up on the right. And you 'Rice Crispies'," as he called the Roman Catholics (and then he would spit noisily onto the ground), "you line up on the left!"

Actually there was great interest in all things religious for us boys, because most of the time we were starving hungry, thanks to the military intention to keep us lean and mean. Well, the Protestant padre cottoned on to this and at his midweek chaplain's hour he would lay on a plate of biscuits. Very soon Sergeant Partington noticed that his line of Rice Crispies was diminishing fast! "Wait a minute! You, boy. You're a Rice Crispy, aren't you? What are you doing there?"

"No, Sergeant," the boy would respond, looking very offended, "I've been converted." This caused our sergeant some bemusement, but the Catholic priest caught on pretty soon and began offering cakes. Thus began a back-and-forth movement between the major denominations, based on offerings of free food.

Sergeant Partington became a real father figure to me and to several others as well, and we became very close. When he had special events on in the sergeants' mess or functions to attend in the evening he would sometimes ask Dave and me to babysit his children for him in the married quarters. He basically welcomed me into his family, and that meant a lot. I responded well to the kind of approach that he took with me – not that he was gentle or weak in any way, but he was respectful and, above all, fair. That counted for a lot in my mind at that stage of my life, as I sought to find the kind of fathering that I desperately longed for. The senior NCOs were not the monsters we had expected them to be.

The Junior Leaders was very much as I imagine public school to be, with its system of prefects and discipline imposed by those just ahead of you. The guys who ranked as NCOs among the Junior Leaders were usually only a few months

41

older than us and they brutalized us, hitting and degrading us whenever they could.

They invented horrors like "quick change parade", where during the night they would yell at us and get us out of bed to stand to attention in the corridor. We were usually still half asleep and clasping our hands around ourselves in a kind of "cross your heart" action, just trying to wake up and find comfort at one and the same time. Then they would scream, "Get changed into an NBC kit (Nuclear Biological and Chemical) NOW! – and you've got thirty seconds to do it in!" Well, it was impossible to do the task they were demanding of us, so they would make us run around with our mess tin on our head or strapped to our private parts, and this went on all night long, so we often got no sleep.

The purpose of all this, other than to serve their twisted fantasies, was to break us, and it worked – many of the guys simply dropped out and went home. All recruits hit a wall at some point in their basic training and ask themselves, "Is this for me or not?" There was a moment about the two-month point when I hit that wall too, and I might have gone home if things had not turned out differently for me in a remarkable and unexpected way.

5

HITTING THE WALL

Despite the difficult early weeks I was quite a determined soldier. I was physically fit and for me the brutality was sadly nothing new. During the first few weeks I was beaten up by an NCO from Manchester but I had been prepared for that by the things I had heard about life in the army. There were moments when I would write home saying, "I miss home" or "I miss you guys", but it never meant much apart from being a little homesick, mostly for my mother's love and her food.

The lowest point for me came after the first month or so. It was over a weekend when other guys were away, many of them at their homes, that I began to question whether or not I could go on. Sergeant Partington spotted that I was struggling and spoke to me, encouraging me not to give up, but he and I both knew that the decision would be mine alone in the end.

The turning point for me came the following week when we went on an exercise up on the Yorkshire moors just outside Catterick. I had joined up as a January recruit, and throughout the British Army the January intake was infamous because of the appalling kinds of weather they had to endure. On this occasion it was freezing cold and the rain, sleet, and snow were lashing down mercilessly. We were still raw recruits and the conditions were taking a heavy toll on us all.

A couple of the guys were stricken with the final stages of hypothermia and had to be evacuated off the moors. We operated a "buddy" system of twinning boys up to watch out for each other, and once lads began to freeze almost to death it was put into urgent action. We were ordered to get into a sleeping bag with each suffering soldier and hug him close in order to impart our body heat to him, taking it in turns so as not to deplete our own meagre resources too far. Once they realized that some recruits' lives were in real danger, the senior NCOs arranged for their urgent removal for medical care.

There was no such reprieve for me or for many of us as we struggled with the elements on that bleak and windswept mountainside. After several hours of these almost Arctic conditions we were ordered to dig trenches in the freezing ground. The effort it took to make any kind of indentation in earth like reinforced concrete was almost beyond me. My fingers were throbbing with cold and there was a long icicle forming on the end of my nose. Then, just as we thought we had done the impossible and produced what we thought were decent trenches, the instructors described them as pathetic scrapings and ordered us to fill them all in again!

By that time everyone was just lying around shattered because there was no fight left in them. I remember the instructors then saying, "We don't get off this mountainside until you've filled in those trenches", and at that moment a red mist came down over my frozen brain. It wasn't long since I'd had my chat with Sergeant Partington, and something in me just snapped. I flipped and grabbed the pickaxe and shovel nearest to me, and started to go berserk. I ran around the trenches like a thief escaping from the police, grabbing the other recruits as I went. I shook them and yelled at them, saying, "Come on, let's do this! You heard the officer! Get these trenches filled in! I'm not staying here any longer!"

With this I set to like a maniac to fill in each trench myself. I was out of my mind with anger, frustration, cold, and fatigue, and cared about nothing more than getting down off that mountain and into the warm. The sweat began to form on my back and almost immediately to turn to ice as I exerted myself like a man possessed. I didn't care what anyone thought of me; I just wanted down off that moor. Gradually the other recruits began to join me in the Herculean task before us, and within a short time the job was done.

What I did not realize then in my manic state was that all this had impressed the instructors. They thought, "Ah, Gilvear's in the zone now. He's becoming a real soldier!" This is what they wanted – motivation but to the extreme – and from that moment on I became a good soldier, at least in their minds. When I got back off that exercise I was promoted – for going berserk! They said, "Gilvear has clearly got leadership qualities", and they made me up to lance corporal.

Even my instructor of military training, Corporal Garnet, who will remain in my memory for ever as "the devil incarnate", couldn't believe it and asked, "What happened to you up there?"

"I don't know, Corporal, but at least it got the job done, eh?" I replied slyly.

From that moment everything changed. That was the day I became a man. First I was promoted to lance corporal and then not long afterwards to full corporal. Then I was earmarked as one of the four potential sergeants, the highest rank you could attain as a Junior Leader at that time. Only one recruit would make it to sergeant out of the whole intake. Whoever did would be regarded as the best of the best, and all four of us who were full corporals were hoping for that one slot, and me more than anyone. I was really hungry for acceptance and advancement. I longed for someone in authority to say, "Well done, son. You are the best." At one stage I really thought I had it in the bag. I was performing well, and my drill was really good because I had no problem with shouting at people. Whenever I was given a task to do I did it – well, most of the time, anyway. And I loved it.

All was going well, except that I began to recognize that alcohol was becoming a bit of a problem for me. As Junior Leaders, we were strictly speaking not allowed to drink, because we were still underage. Yet despite that the army seemed to make up its own rules as it went along, since after each event that we won – manoeuvres, competitions, and so on – we would receive crates of beer as a reward. Bradley Squadron, my squadron, and Lightning Troop, my platoon, were regular winners of the log race or the assault course and other events, so the beer soon started to flow fairly freely, with official sanction. It nearly became my undoing.

I will never forget an incident when alcohol nearly destroyed my chances of being promoted any higher. Sergeant Major Duncan Williamson was a Scots Guardsman who put the fear of death into everyone, although to me he was just a typical hard-nosed Scot from Port Glasgow, and in many ways a character just like my dad. He was a fearsome beast of a man in his peaked cap with split peaks, in the manner of the Guards, and wherever he went he was always marching, whether he had his pace stick or not.

He used methods of discipline that were unique to him and which would not be appropriate in today's army. The sergeant major had this thing about any recruit that he caught "going sick". He believed that if you went on sick parade, for anything at all, you were not a man. If he saw you at the Health Centre he would chase you out before you had been seen by a medic! It didn't even matter if you had pneumonia – he would burst into the waiting room yelling, "Get out of here! You don't need medication!" and he was just crazy.

He had his very own process of dealing with soldiers who did wrong. He wouldn't bother with paperwork and filing a charge if they had committed any offence contrary to military standards or discipline. He would say, "You have a choice, laddie. You can take my punishment or you can take the army's. It's up to you."

It was no light matter to fall into the hands of Sergeant Major Williamson, but, strangely, most defaulters chose his medicine rather than the army's. We called his office "Dunkie Williamson's Mean Machine Room". If you walked past his office any time and you saw that the blinds were closed, you knew someone was in there and trembled at the thought. Inside that frightful office he would take his pace stick and whack it on the desk and if he so decided he would whack the offender with it! Recruits would sometimes stumble out holding their heads, but that was the matter dealt with. He did not seem to hold on to any resentment afterwards, but it was a fearsome regime to live under.

Strangely, I actually loved him. I could recognize the Scottish character he was playing and that deep down he was a decent man. Occasionally he would wink at me as if to say "There's a Scottish link, isn't there, eh?" and I felt I understood him. There was a downside to this, though, because he was even more convinced that no Scottish recruit could go sick! "Ye cannae be sick, mon; ye're Scottish!" he would cry in sheer disbelief at such a thing, beating me about the head as he chased me from the Health Centre even before the pretty nurse had had time to triage me.

After a few months I was still a lance corporal and my best friend, Dave Pilling, was also a lance corporal. We were very close, but we were both pushing for the single post of sergeant, which I dearly wanted. I don't think Dave was really that bothered, but it meant so much to me in my driven state of mind. We were about to be promoted to full corporal, and towards the end of a working week we were asked to go to the NAAFI (a shop and bar for junior ranks in the barracks where most of our social occasions, centred around food and drink, took place) to get some boot polish for the recruits under our care. It was evening time after the meal and the lads needed to get their kit ready for the Sunday parade, so, as trusted junior NCOs who were deemed responsible, we were the ones tasked by the instructors with obtaining the polish. Recruits used a lot of boot polish, as you can imagine, and it was also used on the barrack-room floors, where we would apply it with our hands and knees and then buff it with electric bumpers. So we collected the money from the boys and went off to get the polish. What should have taken only ten minutes unfortunately became a whole night of mayhem, and the lads never got their polish! When we arrived at the NAAFI store we saw the bar there and Dave asked me, "Do you fancy a beer?" By that stage I had developed a real taste for it, and we were arrogant about our task and position. So we had a beer, and then another one and another, and soon we were plastered. We thought we were untouchable, once the beer was flowing. Then we sang loudly all the way back to the barrack block, where by now the recruits for whom we were responsible were in bed. Rummaging in the cupboards we found the big electric bumper machines for keeping the floors so clean and we drove them all over the place, scattering their kit and basically just smashing up their area. Dave had hold of the handles and I was squatting on the machine itself, which we used to do in order to add weight when they were in proper use. The recruits were under our command, but here we were, drunk as skunks, breaking up their barrack room or "lines", as we called them. Horrified and terrified recruits screamed like banshees and jumped out of bed, fleeing such a scene of chaos.

This farce went on until the Regimental Military Police showed up, alerted by the recruits that we were trashing their lines. They grabbed us harshly and then marched us over to the jail. I was thrown into one cell and Dave was put in another nearby. I could hear him shouting out to me, "Bill! Don't tell them anything. They're spies, they're Russians, don't give anything away!" This was still the time of the Cold War and we were taught to be very wary of spies and agents, but he was off his head with paranoia caused by the drink. I groaned, "Oh, Dave, shut up! We're already in so much trouble, mate. Don't make it any worse!"

The next morning Company Sergeant Major Williamson himself crashed into the jailhouse to collect us. I thought to myself, "Oh boy, we're dead, and I'm busted. I've lost my rank now. I'm really in trouble here." In full CSM regalia he marched us across the parade ground at the double so that everyone could see us.

"Left right left right, stop there. Mark time!" he yelled for the entire world to hear. He was doing what we called "beasting" –

making a spectacle of us on the square for everyone to behold. We obeyed like automatons, fearing for our futures. Then he marched us right over and into his office and, ominously, he pulled down the blinds. We were dead meat!

He looked at us both and said slowly, "Now, what do you want, boys? Do we do it the army way or my way?" We were shaking in our shoes, but there was no question of which way we would go.

"Your way, Sergeant Major," I said weakly, trembling. All he did was bring his pace stick down on the desktop with a deafening crack and say, "I depend on you two. I like you. Now get out there and don't let me ever catch you doing this sort of nonsense again."

We ran outside as fast as we could and did not stop until we were well away from Dunkie Williamson's "Mean Machine". Once out of sight we just collapsed onto each other with relief and laughter. We could not believe it but we kept our rank, and three days later Dave and I and two others were promoted to full corporal! We had messed up so badly, but had been given another chance. But – ominously – the underlying message that I absorbed into my subconscious in all this was that drunken foolishness is forgivable in the army. That was a dangerous assumption for me and one that would come back again and again to bite me until my very character would be chewed up and spat out by it. In fact, it nearly killed me.

6

GROWING UP FAST

Looking back on that encounter with Dunkie Williamson's Mean Machine, I realize that if I had been busted my life might have turned out very differently. After going berserk up on the Yorkshire moors and being promoted, followed by the sheer madness of my drunken rampage and subsequent immunity from punishment, I began to get an understanding of what my new life demanded. The army was giving me the impression that a soldier needed to be brutal, really hard, and if that involved getting drunk occasionally and being stupid, that was just fine within its context of authority and leadership.

I really think that if I hadn't gone into the army I would have ended up as a young offender, because that moment on the Yorkshire moors when I flipped could very well have happened in civilian life. There would have come a point when I snapped, and perhaps even hurt somebody, and I would probably have been arrested. The army could contain that sort of behaviour, though, and in fact they loved it – even causing it to happen.

Now things have changed, of course, because of the tragic deaths of some young recruits. An independent report into the

51

mysterious deaths of four young recruits at Deepcut Barracks between 1995 and 2002 exposed a culture of bullying, sexual abuse, and sadism concerning young recruits.[3] Today the advent of the "health and safety society" and the trend towards a generally more litigious way of life have brought about major reforms. Change was needed, in my opinion, simply on the grounds of basic humanity, but in my day, and even up to the 1990s, anything went.

This became very real for me during my first month of army life, when I was brutally beaten up by a senior instructor for falling asleep in his lecture. As recruits we were up all night many nights and got very little sleep. A corporal from Manchester was giving us a lecture on nuclear, biological, and chemical warfare (NBC) and we had to stay awake as this was an important lesson for us, particularly because at that time (during the Cold War) we were concerned about the very real possibility of imminent nuclear attack.

I knew that, but I was exhausted and I started to nod off. Suddenly I was shocked awake by a heavy blow to my head, and afterwards the other lads told me what had happened. The instructor took a heavy rifle, an SLR (Self-Loading Rifle), held it over me with the metal muzzle pointing down at my head, and motioned for everyone to be quiet. The SLR had been used by the British Army for about thirty years at that point and was in the process of being phased out in favour of the smaller SA80 assault rifle, but it was still in use among training units. It was much bigger than the more modern rifles and weighed around 4.5 kilograms (nearly 10 pounds). He held it over me for a few seconds and then let this weapon fall down on top of me with a mighty bang, splitting my head

3   http://www.independent.co.uk/opinion/leading-articles/a-shameful-chapter-in-the-history-of-the-british-army-728676.html

open. Immediately I awoke in shock and pain, with blood pouring down my face, but he didn't stop there. He started kicking me in the groin, aiming for my crotch, smashing me with kick after kick. My chair flew back and the other recruits scattered in terror.

"Don't you ever ****ing fall asleep in my lecture again, you little s***!" screamed the instructor. "Get outta here and get your head sorted!"

I picked myself up and headed straight for the door. Clutching my head, I ran over to the Health Centre to get stitches, hoping that Sergeant Major Williamson wouldn't come in on one of his rampages. As soon as the stitches were in and my head wound was cleaned up I was told to rejoin my troop straight away, and I did so without delay. I have to say that I never fell asleep in a lecture again! The instructors actually taught us techniques to avoid that: pinching your leg if you thought you were nodding off, and learning how to breathe properly. There was no way I was ever going to do that again.

But the message of brutality was being reinforced for me. I was becoming a very aggressive and violent young man myself. Today I expect that instructor would be disciplined if not prosecuted, but back then sadistic violence was just a cultural expectation in the armed forces.

7

DAY OF PRIDE

Graduation from the Junior Leaders was a fantastic occasion for me, and took place in December at the end of my first year. The day itself meant a huge parade, and I had received that highly coveted promotion to sergeant so I was out in the front, with Company Sergeant Major (CSM) Williamson in overall command. The whole trade college was there, together with everyone in the Junior Leaders barracks, dignitaries from Harrogate, and some general whose name I can't remember who was taking the salute. A massive day from the off, with the big mixed band, pipes and drums, and there I was out in front with my very own pace stick and a sash, leading Lightning Troop out of training. It was a very proud moment and I still have it on video. My family were there to witness it all and there I was bawling out the commands: "Left Turn, Right Turn, and Halt!" I knew that I had achieved something worthwhile. I had become the best of the best.

One of those attending the parade was a Major Fisher, who was actually a big influence on my life at Harrogate. CSM Williamson found him frustrating because he was a real cricket fan, a member of the famous Middlesex Cricket Club (MCC), and a bit of a toff really, but Major Fisher spotted the potential in me and urged me to make the most of my opportunity in the army. He was possibly one of the five most significant men in my whole life. He was the most pastorally minded man I'd met up to that point and he was big in stature and well educated, with a great command of the English language. His inspirational talks before we went off on any exercises were always based on Winnie the Pooh, and he managed to get some really profound quotes from Pooh Bear that sent us off buzzing with amusement and a desire to succeed. It was bizarre really. But he was a genius with the English language. He amazed me when he took me aside at one point and said that he believed I would one day make an officer. That was still quite fresh in my mind as I led my troop around the square at graduation like some strutting cock, yelling out orders in my best parade-ground voice. After that, I found myself being posted off into the regular army, and this time as a very junior soldier again, without rank. My record followed me, however, and everywhere I went after that first year my service record flagged me up as a potential leader.

Initially after graduation I was sent to Catterick in Yorkshire again, this time to join the 8th Signals Regiment in order to learn a trade, which in my case was that of radio operator. In the army anyone with a trade is still first of all a soldier and has to learn how to use a rifle and fight, but it was also deemed appropriate for us to learn other skills so as to be as useful as possible.

Arriving at Catterick was not as dramatic as it had been in Harrogate for the Junior Leaders. At least I was sober this time. When we entered through the barracks gate there was nobody screaming and shouting at us because by that stage we were being treated as mature soldiers. Mind you, although the hierarchy did not give us such a hard time, the other serving soldiers did. Once I had arrived at my billet they demanded to know where I was from, and all of a sudden I realized that I was a small fish in a very big pond. I also felt my youth keenly again, as I was still only seventeen, and small in stature.

Once settled in at Catterick I was called into the office and stood ramrod straight at attention while the officer at the desk perused his notes for a few minutes. Then he looked up.

"I've been reading your record, Gilvear," he said laconically. All kinds of dark thoughts went through my mind at that moment. Did he know about my drunken exploits beginning on day one at Harrogate and continuing even up to when I was a junior NCO myself?

"Yes, Sir!" I snapped, dying inside.

"Relax, boy," he muttered, looking back at the sheaf of papers. "You've got a great record from your beginnings in basic training and we're going to be really watching you as a potential officer. How do you feel about that?"

"Yes, Sir. Thank you, Sir," I replied mechanically, though deeply relieved and somewhat surprised.

"Well, that means that in addition to your trade training we will be giving you some special tasks and you will also be responsible for groups of men at drill. I read here that you have a strong voice and clear parade-ground awareness. I know you are still young but we will be keeping an eye on you for possible promotion. Do you understand?"

"Yes, thank you, Sir".

"Don't thank me, laddie; you sound like some kind of tape recorder!"

"Sir!" I barked at the top of my voice, saluting and performing a smart about-turn and marching out of his office. Inwardly I was delighted, because this suited my driven nature and my longing for approval from those above me.

At Catterick I searched for ways of becoming accepted by the older men among whom I found myself. Quite quickly I realized that drinking beer was an important part of the barracks culture, and I entered into this with relish. What I didn't realize then, of course, was that for these guys alcohol wasn't a problem but for me it would eventually become a real concern. I didn't think I was using alcohol for any other reason than for having a good time with the guys, but they knew how to stop and I was fast finding out that I did not. During my time at 8th Signals I began to experience some really heavy drinking sessions. It was amazing that I was able to do this when I was only seventeen and still underage, but I was soon to be eighteen and I was in the big boys' army, so neither the law nor the future mattered much to me.

8

P COMPANY

That year in Catterick passed swiftly and I was posted to a Signals section in 5 Airborne Brigade in Aldershot as a radio operator. I was there for nearly a year and while there I got my driving licence and achieved my Heavy Goods Vehicle (HGV) licence too, and in doing so had great fun. For a while I worked for the Blue Helmets, an elite parachute display team, as ground crew. Once again it was put down on my record that I was expected to go far, and I had a lot of responsibility for my age. Following that spell of duty supporting the Blue Helmets it became one of my dreams to undertake the all-arms Pegasus Company (P Coy) course, which is a parachute selection course famed for its rigour and high standards. Potential Parachute Regiment soldiers and any member of the armed forces wishing to join an Air Assault Brigade even today must go through Pre-Parachute Selection (PPS) run by the Parachute Regiment (P Company), which was then held in Aldershot but has since relocated to Catterick.

I arrived there full of excitement, fear, and exhilaration. I knew that the course would be tough, but had no idea what was about to hit me. When we were settling in, the NCO in charge of our section gave us all a leaflet containing an outline of the eight tests that we would need to succeed in during the ensuing weeks if we were to pass P Company. If any of these were failed or we were unable to perform them within the stipulated times and conditions, we would be sent packing. I was desperate to pass, but as I scanned the eight tests my heart was in my mouth. The leaflet read as follows:

The Eight Tests in P Coy

10-miler

A 10-mile (16 km) march conducted as a squad over undulating terrain. Each candidate carries a 35 lb (16 kg) bergen[4] (not including water) and a rifle. The march is currently to be completed in less than one hour fifty minutes. (I realized that would require an average marching speed of nearly 6 mph/9.6 kph heavily laden!)

The Trainasium

A unique assault course set 60 feet (18 m) above the ground, designed to test a candidate's ability to both overcome fear and follow simple orders at considerable height. This is the only event that is a straight pass or fail; all the other events are scored. The total score required to pass is known only to the P Coy staff. (With this one they used to yell up at you just when you were about to leap over a gap or launch out to walk on a long narrow pole 60 feet (18 m) up in the air – they wanted to see if you would obey without question or hesitation. Obviously many did not.)

4   Military rucksack.

The Log Race

A team event, in which eight men carry a log (which was actually a telegraph pole) weighing 132 lb (60 kg) over 1.9 miles (3.1 km) of undulating terrain. Candidates wear a helmet and webbing. (This was supposed to be one of the hardest events – and it was.)

2-Mile March

An individual effort over 2 miles (3.2 km) of undulating terrain, carrying a 35 lb (16 kg) bergen (not including water), rifle, combat jacket, and helmet. Candidates have eighteen minutes to complete the run. (An average speed of nearly 7 mph/11 kph!)

The Steeplechase

A timed, 1.8-mile (2.9 km) cross-country run, followed by an assault course. The time limit is nineteen minutes, after which candidates lose one point every thirty seconds.

Milling

In this event, each candidate is paired with another of similar weight and build, and is given sixty seconds to demonstrate "controlled physical aggression" in a milling contest – similar to boxing, except neither winning, losing, nor skill are prerequisites for passing. Candidates are instead scored on their determination, while blocking and dodging result in points being deducted. Candidates will wear boxing gloves. (Today they also are allowed to use head protection and gum shields as well as boxing gloves. This was sheer madness, a blur of pain. The guys they matched me with always seemed so much bigger than me. It did not seem fair. I just hit out like some kind of cartoon character in a blur of blows. Usually the big opponent got the better of me, but I scored high for energy and effort.)

20-Mile Endurance March

A 20-mile (32 km) squad march over diverse types of terrain. Candidates carry a 35 lb (16 kg) bergen (not including water) and a rifle. The march must be completed in less than four hours and thirty minutes. (This was an absolute killer, as we were mostly sleep-deprived and starving hungry. The lower average speed of 4.5 mph/7 kph was offset by the sheer exhaustion caused by the extreme distance.)

Stretcher Race

Candidates are divided into teams of sixteen men, and have to carry a 175 lb (79 kg) stretcher over a distance of 5 miles (8.0 km), with each individual candidate wearing a helmet, webbing, and a slung rifle. No more than four candidates carry the stretcher at any given time, swapping round at regular intervals so that all candidates carry the stretcher for a certain distance. (I remember even now the agony of holding on to my allotted handle and marching in double time longing for the instructor to yell "Swap now!")

At the start of this period in my life both my physical fitness and my endurance were at an exceptional level. I could run for ever. I wasn't big but I was like a wiry little greyhound, and I just kept on going. One of the selection tests, the steeplechase, required us to run a few miles through a forest down in Aldershot. At various intervals they had placed logs of wood as obstacles designed to slow us down or trip us up. I broke the record for that and my time stood for a couple of years. My attitude was that it wasn't the taking part that was important – it was succeeding and being the best. I was still trying so hard to please the instructors, and whenever I powered across the finishing line first it meant that I got to hear those treasured words "Well done, laddie!" I didn't realize it then, of course, but it was feeding my need for approval from authority figures.

Because I loved to hear that kind of commendation I was willing to put up with anything the instructors put my way. When it came to the "milling" they told us to assemble in the gym, and once there we sat down in the shape of a large square on the floor. Then they numbered us as we yelled out our own place in the sequence one by one. I think I was number 37, and then they said, "Right, number 37, Gilvear – come on; get into the ring." So I stood up and moved into the middle with my oversized gloves on and I remember thinking, "These gloves are bigger than me!" Then they selected someone who they said was a similar size to me but was actually a real Goliath, shouting that we had two minutes, and then we were expected to knock lumps out of each other. As this milling exercise took place in Test Week it was vital to do well, and the instructors were watching like hawks. The point was that they wanted to see courage, evidenced by the fact that neither fighter would quit no matter how much blood was shed. I certainly shed some that day but I had to be dragged off my opponent. I was all over him like an angry rash. I remember that the guy I faced was huge, which seemed so unfair, but I began to dig deep within myself, thinking about my beginnings and how I had come to where I was, and I was determined not to be beaten.

I recall being knocked about on that awful day but actually thriving on it! There was blood everywhere and even after the two minutes were up the instructors had to pull me off this guy. As they tried to drag us apart they were saying, "Right, Gilvear, stop. That's it; no more!" I didn't hear either the bell or their voices because I was in a blaze of rage and energy, my arms milling like a machine, raining blows on my opponent. I was like Scrappy Doo[5] with blood everywhere; it was a truly surreal moment but I really enjoyed it.

It was during one of these dreadful tests that I broke my ankle. I was young and energetic and determined to pass P Company so I forced myself to carry on without getting the necessary attention for my ankle. As a result the injury became a problem that would hound me for the rest of my army career and beyond.

We were doing a series of warming-up exercises early in the morning in a part of the Aldershot training area. We hadn't got to the final test phase yet and we were sent to a place called Long Valley, not far from the barracks. It is used mainly for tracked vehicles such as tanks and armoured cars, which tear up the ground mercilessly. The terrain is quite undulating and when it rains it becomes a swamp. When the weather is dry the ground becomes really hard and dusty, like some bleak Afghan landscape, but it was winter when we were there so it was frozen hard. We were doing fireman's lifts, where you get one of your buddies on your back and then run up and down

5   Scrappy Cornelius Doo is a fictional Great Dane puppy cartoon character created by Hanna–Barbera Productions in 1979. With a highly energetic and brave personality, despite his small size, Scrappy was the exact opposite of his uncle, the famous Scooby Doo; Scrappy would usually insist on trying to fight the various monsters Scooby and his associates encountered and generally have to be dragged away by Scooby. Source http://en.wikipedia.org/wiki/Scrappy-Doo

a steep embankment. The idea was to carry them up and drop them off at the top, then run back down, where you change round and they carry you up. On this occasion I got to the top carrying one of my mates and was quite fatigued, so I was not being as careful as I would normally try to be. I turned around, dropping my load, came running down the embankment, and went over on my ankle on the uneven ground.

Hearing it go "crack" straight away, I let out a loud yelp and went down in a heap. I was breathing heavily and starting to feel dizzy. The medics were called over and they could not ascertain straight away if it was a break, but my ankle was swollen like a snake that had swallowed a grapefruit. I could hardly walk so they put me in the back of a Land Rover. It was just a warming-up session so there was no failure involved, at least not yet, but my heart was in my boots, fearing the worst. The medics took me back to camp where they applied ice to my ankle, gave me the magic pink tablets (ibuprofen, I think), and elevated my foot to rest it. I was feeling really sorry for myself but in the army there is no sympathy. At first the instructors came in and thought I was faking it. They reckoned the whole thing was too hard for me and I wanted to quit, but nothing could have been further from the truth. When one of them bent down to unwrap the bandage around my ankle, though, he said, "Sorry, mate. Your P Company is over", but I replied, "No way, Corporal. I'm not going through all this again." Of course at my young age I had plenty of time to do the whole course again, but there was no way anyone would put themselves through that kind of punishment more than once if they had a choice. And I did have a choice, because it was left up to me.

These days I think the health and safety brigade would have forbidden me to go on, and they would probably have been doing me a favour. At that time, though, when I did see the doctor he just shrugged and said, "Do whatever you want to, son, but that's a break." So I rested that weekend because we were off duty and I forced myself through the pain barrier and just went on. In the middle of the following week I went for an X-ray because it still wasn't settling down, and it showed that there was a hairline fracture of the ankle. Once again the choice was mine and I decided to carry on. I was young and fit so I ran through it – it is amazing what you can do when you are highly motivated. Maybe at that age there is something in your physique that enables you to overcome things more easily, so I did. But the ankle became a huge problem later.

Throughout my career from then on I would get severe pain in that ankle without warning. I could go over on it very easily and I used to do so regularly, often causing concern among my coaches and superiors. The reason for my running through the pain and not dealing with it at P Company was not just that I didn't want to go through the tests again but also that I liked the fact that the instructors said, "Well done, Gilvear, you're really going for this again even with a broken ankle." It was clear that they respected me for this even more than before. I so wanted to please but it became a real hindrance to me, a bit of a thorn in the flesh. There were times when I would play football or rugby and go over on it and be out of the game. It affected me continually over the years and I wasn't really able to do what I could have done had I rested and had the broken ankle properly set. When I did eventually leave the army it was on the grounds of a medical discharge because of my ankle.

At the end of Test Week at P Company we gathered in the mess hall to be given the news, good or bad. I was amazed when some guys failed who had seemed really capable to me. The officer commanding (OC) read out the names one by one: "Macpherson (the candidate stood) – fail."

"Yes, Sir," he muttered, utterly dejected.

"Jones – fail."

"Yes, Sir."

"Gilvear…" (I hauled myself to my feet) – "Pass!" You could hear the surprise in his voice, which matched my own.

"Yes, Sir!" I yelled in triumph. I could hardly believe it. Despite being the youngest there, and breaking my ankle, I had passed what was a massive and demanding physical endurance test highly regarded by members of all the armed forces. I had made it. I felt accepted. Sadly, my ankle problem meant that I could not go on to RAF Brize Norton to undertake the further parachute training that would have earned me my wings. But I knew I was up to the mark.

9

A SCOTTISH SOLDIER

At this point in my army career I decided to transfer to a Scottish regiment. These units are renowned for their fierce fighting skills and aggression and are often given romantic portrayals in the popular media. Their "Scottishness" is not necessarily due to recruitment in Scotland alone or to any set proportion of soldiers having Scottish ancestry, but many of their recruits are Scots, like me. Traditionally, Scottish regiments have their headquarters north of the border and often adopt tartan colours, kilts, and pipe bands as part of their culture. I joined the Argyll and Sutherland Highlanders, known as "the Argylls".

I had to go through infantry training at Glencorse Barracks. It was located in Penicuik, a burgh in Midlothian to the south of Edinburgh, on the west bank of the River North Esk, and was formerly used as an infantry training centre. It has now been developed into a modern and attractive example of military housing, but in those days it was a crumbling and depressing sight with its ancient crenellated towers and austere blocks of accommodation much in need of restoration.

Glencorse was, however, a thriving centre of the Scottish Division. Soon I was wearing the kilt and the full regalia of my home regiment. Its headquarters were at Stirling Castle, very near where I used to live, and some of the guys I met there had been at school with me. There was a real feeling of local community about the outfit, and some of the soldiers had fathers and uncles in the regiment, or their grandfathers had served in it.

I had to go through specialist infantry training at Glencorse Barracks. We sharpened up on becoming infantry soldiers in particular, laying aside our trade activities as secondary. We were to become "cannon fodder" – a term dating from the time when the infantry were at the front of the battle lines as the cannon balls were fired. To avoid becoming cannon fodder we had to get to grips with topics such as interpreting firing orders, marksmanship, escape and evasion, and renewing our levels of aggression, which are all part of the skills the modern infantry soldier has to develop in order to survive when the day of battle finally comes.

At Glencorse we spent a lot of time on the ranges, shooting and zeroing in our weapons. Previously that had been done by an instructor, who would talk us through the firing of the sighting rounds and then adjust our sights for us, but now we had to know how to do all that ourselves. The attitude was "Well, you're an infantry soldier now so you do it yourself". There was a constant drive to arouse aggression in us, and never more so than during bayonet practice.

Aggression comes from the flow of adrenaline into a highly trained and prepared individual. All through my military career instructors yelled and screamed at us to show more fighting spirit, never more so than during my infantry training. The bayonet is a cruel piece of military kit and is basically a metal dagger, around 20 cm (8 inches) in length, which clips on to the muzzle of a rifle or light machine gun. It is designed for close-quarters fighting or perhaps a situation where a soldier's ammunition has run out and the enemy is still closing with him. This actually happened as recently as 2009, when Lieutenant James Adamson, aged twenty-four, of the Royal Regiment of Scotland, was awarded the Military Cross for a bayonet charge while on a tour of duty in Afghanistan.

So we were all trained in the use of the bayonet. This training would often take place on a rifle range or outdoor exercise area, far away from prying eyes. Instructors seemed to delight in explaining all the gory details about the bayonet, including the purpose of its serrated edge, which is for cutting bone and sinew, and the little channel in the blade formed to allow blood to escape back from the wound and air to enter so that the blade can be withdrawn. Once the trainees have mastered the physical act of drawing and fixing bayonets they then have to learn how to use them. We were usually made to stand at the ready – with weapons held in both hands and bayonets fixed. We were taught how to go "on guard" with our weapon, crouching and screaming as we thrust our bayonets forward again and again. We would be made to march on the spot, chanting "Kill, kill, kill!" over and over. An NCO would yell, "What is the bayonet for?" and we would all scream back the chant: "Kill, kill, kill!" Or another instructor would call, "What makes the grass grow?" and we were ordered to reply by yelling out, "Blood, blood, blood!" with a blood-curdling degree of ferocity.

By this time we were usually in a frenzy of anticipation and aggression, pulses racing and neck veins bulging. I am sure that any sensible enemy would have been long gone. Then it was on down the range, rushing and screaming madly at the same time. We were expected to plunge our bayonets into sandbags on the ground or tethered to makeshift poles or formed into stuffed dummies to represent real people. I did this with all the energy I could muster, stabbing and hacking at the make-believe enemy like a crazy wildcat tearing at its prey. I loved the feeling of it, the noise, the aggression, and the rush of power it gave me.

On one occasion, though, while I was still in the Scottish Division of infantry, bayonet practice comprised most of the above plus an almost unbelievable extra. We were led down the range and told to put our weapons down in a certain order so that we would be able to find them again quickly. The NCOs had laid out a rope circle, perhaps a few metres across, and set it down on the ground. We were ordered to stand around the circle facing inwards.

On the order "Move!" we had to throw ourselves into the circle and begin beating the living daylights out of each other en masse until there was only one of us standing! Groaning, but not daring to disobey, we leapt forward at the word of command and started laying into one another crazily. The instructors stood around the rope circle yelling abuse and urging us on in the pursuit of blood and victory. Some guys were actually punched senseless, which seemed to defeat the object of the exercise, which was to stir up aggression in us. Mark McPherson, a huge ex-farmer from Thurso in Scotland, a member of the Queen's Own Highlanders, grabbed me with his massive, meaty arms like a butcher hauling a side of beef, and threw me to the ground. He punched and kicked me for what seemed like an age before the whistle was blown to stop this madness. Suddenly this steamed-up heap of brawling infantrymen were ordered up to collect their weapons and charge the target dummies again! Several of them were so stupefied from receiving blows to the head that they could not even see the targets. I could just about see mine, but could not run in a straight line. There was no shortage of aggression but it did not always seem to be very well managed.

Once the exercise was over, however, we were simply marched off back to the base for our meal and as usual found ourselves in the bar that evening getting increasingly drunk and, once again, aggressive. No wonder. This was what the army wanted to see in us. They called it the "killer instinct" and I had it in full measure.

Then, six months into my training at Glencorse, we were posted to Minden in Germany to join my battalion as part of the British Army of the Rhine (BAOR). That turned out to be a really great two years of experience, but it did not start out well at all.

10

DON'T MENTION THE WAR!

Like the lead character in the 1970s BBC television comedy series *Fawlty Towers*, I went to Germany determined not to mention the Second World War yet expecting to encounter some resistance to us just because we were British soldiers. Our camp in Germany had been a Nazi SS base at one time and still had their insignia on the side of the buildings.

Now it was no longer occupied by Hitler's storm troopers the Argylls were billeted there, and I don't know which the people of the area found the more difficult to deal with. Our tour was a very heavy-drinking, hard-working, but aggressive trip. Weekends were just like being in Glasgow city centre late on a Friday and Saturday night.

I walked into the barracks via the big gate with its imposing SS eagle pillars on either side and began the search for my block. I was assigned to 6 Platoon B (Bravo) Company, a rifle company, and as I began looking for my accommodation I came round the corner at the allotted place and looked up to the left. To my amazement I saw a rolled mattress come flying out of a window at the very top of this block, perhaps four or five storeys up, with somebody inside it. It launched out from the wall and then plummeted like a sack filled with roofing lead straight to the ground, accompanied by a wild scream from the person inside.

I ran forward to see if I could help him but by the time I got there he had already started to get up, picking out bits of mattress from his hair and swearing like the trooper he was. The guys in my block were drunk and had thrown this new recruit out of the window wrapped in his mattress just to see what would happen! They were leaning out of several windows by this stage, laughing uproariously. He was lucky to have survived the fall as he could easily have been killed, so I was really terrified at the prospect of what I was facing as a newcomer.

Sure enough, as the latest arrival from the UK, I had some pretty horrific initiation and drinking games to go through in order to be accepted as part of the platoon. It was a kind of unofficial but compulsory bonding process and could take the form of anything, from what I had witnessed to drinking at what they called "bucket parties", where bottles of spirits and any alcoholic drink they could find were poured into a large black bin. In went copious amounts of vodka, whisky, brandy, and of course beer, and just to be polite we put in a bit of fruit that we chopped up, some apples and oranges.

This stuff was lethal, and after one such bucket party a guy called Tom McPherson ripped a drainpipe off the side of the barracks wall and used it as a kind of make-believe anti-tank rocket launcher. He was off his head completely and he had a real grudge against officers because he regarded them as being "up themselves", as he would say. So he got hold of a firework rocket and put it into the tube, then launched it against the officers just when they were holding an event in a marquee. He fired this rocket right through the officers' mess at the height of the summer ball!

Needless to say, he got jailed for that. We had our own jail in the Argylls, as all good Scottish regiments dealt with their own in matters of discipline, except in extreme cases, when they would send them to the Military Corrective Training Centre (MCTC). Tom was dealt with locally for the rocket attack but it was not long before the general violence, aggression, and drunken bravado of off-duty life got the better of him and he was sent to the MCTC. Tom served his time and then he ran away to join the French Foreign Legion. He was crazy really, but these were the sort of people I found myself mixing with. The heavy and prolonged use of copious amounts of alcohol did me no good at all and continued to pave the way for my own downfall.

I remember that on another occasion I was out with the boys in a grill bar next to our barracks and we were drunk as usual. We were sitting in a row on bar stools, as in the US TV sitcom *Cheers*,[6] drinking beer and fooling around. Bear McCabe and Tam Johnson were squaring up to a soldier from the Queen's Regiment; things got a bit heated and Tam just took a steak knife and stuck it straight through the guy's hand, pinning it to the bar top, and then calmly asked for another knife for his steak! I was sitting there and through my beer-fogged mind I was thinking, "I can't believe this is happening." Gingerly but bravely he pulled the knife out of his hand without complaint, and went to get himself stitched up. Tam was arrested, of course, by the Military Police, because the barman reported him, but it was a good example of the kind

6   *Cheers* is an American TV sitcom that ran from 1982 to 1993. It was produced by Charles/Burrows/Charles Productions, in association with Paramount Network Television for NBC.

of culture we were part of. Though we were at peace it was like a war zone at times.

During that time in Germany I detached myself completely from my family, so much so that I'd been there for months and still hadn't phoned home. I was just getting on with my life. Well, we were on parade one day and there I was among all these big Scottish soldiers, and by that stage I was thinking, "Hey, I'm one of them now. I've done my initiation and I am one of the boys." We had been on an exercise which was always a badge of honour if your unit performed well, which ours had. Then, as we all stood to attention on parade, Sergeant Major Spud McGregor began to allocate duties for the day.

"McPherson?" he yelled.

"Yes, Sir?"

"You go to the gym today."

"Johnston? You're on driver detail today", and then he called out my name: "Gilvear!"

"Yes, Sir?" I was mortified with embarrassment by what he said next.

"Gilvear – your mother has called. You go to the commanding officer. He wants to see you because your mother's worried about you!"

Well, if the ground could have swallowed me up! The guys all groaned and cat-called till the CSM glared them into silence again. I had to march over to the CO and stand to attention in front of him in his office. In his upper-class drawl he finally said, "I've had a call from your mother, Gilvear, and she's extremely worried about you. You haven't called her since you got here! I am detailing you now to get out and telephone her straight away."

"Sir!" I shouted curtly, saluted, and about-turned, marching out stamping my boots in fine military fashion. Oh, the embarrassment! I could have died of shame at that moment, but I knew that I would never live it down in the barracks. When I went back to the block the guys were sniggering and making telephone noises behind their hands.

"Ring ring," the mimics went, and "How's Mummy?" and "Who's a mummy's boy, then?" and that went on for months afterwards. Anyway, I found one of those yellow German telephone boxes just outside the camp gate and I phoned home. Mum answered with "Oh you've finally phoned, then?" which I thought was pretty obvious really. I asked her why she had called the regiment and she replied that she had thought I wasn't speaking to them any more.

"Mum," I protested, trying really hard to be kind but firm at the same time. "This is the army that I am in. The army does not stop for a soldier to phone his mum. Do you know how bad this looks for me?"

"Well it's just because I care about you, son, that's all," she replied, and I already knew my pleading was in vain. In future I did my best to give her a ring now and again, and anyway the guys in the barrack room never let me forget.

Despite the problems of initiation and the heavy drinking off duty, I soon found that even in the Argylls I was doing very well and was put forward for promotion. In my arrogance I kind of expected to become the best of the best, but of course I would never have said this to any of the lads. I was selected to go to the Brecon Beacons in Wales on an advanced course for junior NCOs and I felt that it was a foregone conclusion that I would do well. Once again there was a tremendous sense of satisfaction when my sergeant major said, "Hey, well done,

Gilvear, top again!" Although we were one regiment and we fought for the same cause when we were together, when we were up against one another in this kind of setting we were really quite competitive.

In my case, however, I was still listening out for a fatherly voice telling me that I was doing well. The CSM provided me with that, so I continued to strive and perform well. I passed the Brecon course with distinction and then after that I was sent to take part in a televized contest called *Combat 90* featuring Emlyn Hughes and Anneka Rice as presenters. The idea was that regiments of the British Army would compete against each other in various tasks to see who would win in the end and who could thus call themselves the best. It was all a bit forced, really, and wasn't a true representation because on any given day any regiment can be the best as they are all very similarly trained, but it created a good atmosphere for the television viewers. At that time, before recent cutbacks in the size of the British Army, a regiment might have consisted of around 900 men. For the purposes of *Combat 90* the best two of every rank were chosen in case one got injured, so we sent two privates, two lance corporals, two full corporals, two sergeants, and a team leader, who was Lieutenant Jamie Dewar. It was amazing to be chosen as part of that team and I remember feeling great again. Mind you, all that was soon dampened by the sheer effort of getting through the *Combat 90* selection process itself. It was done over a French Commando course and it was pretty much hell on earth. The course was located in the Black Forest area of Breisach, Germany. I remember thinking halfway through, "I wish I was rubbish! Why do I always have to be the best? I wish I had been a failure and got nowhere near this assault course." The French Commandos took great pleasure in inflicting pain on us, either directly during our unarmed combat or just by giving us excessive target distances to run. Of course we couldn't understand what they were saying because it was all in French, and they totally abused us most of the time, thinking it highly amusing. Anyway, we got through it and I got my French Commando badge.

After I had done that awful French Commando course Lieutenant Dewar told me that he had been watching me as a potential candidate not just for promotion within the ranks of the enlisted men but for a commission as an officer. I didn't really take it in then because I was going through this French experience, with its demanding regime and foreign food. We ate with the French junior enlisted men in their mess hall. We had coffee and bread for breakfast. The coffee was served from a big pot. Instead of cups, we had clear glass dessert bowls that we had to dip into the big pot. We always had butter for the bread but we didn't always have jam. We used our pocket knives to slice the long loaves of bread that a French private delivered to the little club. He would carry three loaves under each sweat-dampened armpit so that his hands were free to carry the big pot of coffee. I think the sweat added some extra flavour. It seemed to me that everything else we ate contained lentils.

I also remember that in their cookhouse they had a wine machine. I thought, "Man, this would be deadly in our cookhouse back at the Argylls!" You could just go and help yourself to wine any time you liked. Sensing our thoughts, Lieutenant Dewar said, "That's for the French alone. Not for any of you. None of you can touch that wine machine!" To be honest, we were so tired most of the time that we could not have cared less. Anyhow, most of us knew that if we drank we would fail the contest. We did well in the end and my French Commando badge was presented by a pompous French colonel who tried to kiss me on both cheeks when he gave it to me. He was lucky I didn't punch his lights out! The French departed from Breisach in 1997, after which the whole complex was remodelled and converted to civilian use.

Following the adrenaline rush caused by *Combat 90* my service in the ranks took me all over the world, including Northern Ireland. At other times, whether in training or on exercises in Canada, Kenya, or Belize, we worked hard and then we would be given time off (R&R) wherever we were. This usually led to drunken antics, brawls, and spats with the local police, but the army did not really pay much attention to this unless our actions began to affect the good name of the regiment. There was at least one occasion when I was very lucky indeed not to end up in the regimental prison or the military jail in Colchester. My reputation as an animal when drunk was one thing, but I was starting to have a problem containing my anger and aggression even when stone cold sober. Once I was standing around outside a bar in Aldershot, before I had started drinking, and I took offence at the way some local bikers were looking at me. I accused them loudly of disrespect, and worse, and then piled into them with fists flying. I was small but fearless and equipped with a powerful pair of fists, and soon a mass brawl was underway. Two other off-duty soldiers saw what was going down and piled in to help me, with the intention of pulling me away from the fray.

Then the blue lights were flashing and the crowd began to scatter as the local police and the MPs arrived. I staggered away and went off bold as brass to find a pizza. Someone must have identified me to the officers as they followed me along to the pizza parlour and arrested me there. This was serious, as some of the bikers were badly hurt and were being taken away by ambulance. I was taken to the police station where I was thrown into a cell overnight and taken out to be questioned by a detective the next day. Amazingly, when the bikers gave their statements, they described the two soldiers who had come to my aid in detail, but they did not put their finger on me. Taff, one of the two Good Samaritan troopers, was charged and sent to a local military prison. The other was also found guilty of affray, but I was not even charged, even though I had started it! I was developing a real anger problem and an issue with aggression.

Socially, things had got so bad for me in Germany that I had started to get a terrible reputation, to be honest even within my own regiment. I wanted to be the best when it came to my military skills but outside that I had become what some of the guys described as a "disgusting animal". I was very physically violent and the group that I hung around with in the Argylls were known for causing mayhem wherever we went. This became such a big thing for me that when I used to go out on a Friday night the guys in 6 Platoon would ask me where I was going so that they could have their doors locked and barred by the time I came back. On earlier occasions when I had got drunk I had gone into their rooms when I returned the worse for wear and pulled their overhead lockers down even if they were lying underneath them, causing havoc. I used to smash their lockers and trash their possessions, and thought this was funny. Sometimes I also hit them around the head with broom handles and acted as if it was all hilarious. Sadly, because of the drink, I had become an object of fear among my comrades.

Despite these problems, I did *Combat 90* as a lance corporal and during exercises afterwards I was promoted to full corporal. Once again my professional record had followed me and it was not long after we had returned to camp in Germany that my officer commanding called me in and said, "Look, Gilvear, what do you want to do? You know we could promote you again but eventually you are going to run out of options and then what are we going to do with you? How about you consider a commission?"

I remember feeling good about what he was saying, but I was also very torn in my thinking. In the lower ranks of the army there is a real loyalty to the lads training and fighting alongside you. There was also a real cultural division between officers and men, and this was especially the case in the Scottish regiments. If you became an officer you were seen as going over to the other side and betraying your roots.

Officers in the Scottish regiments really were of a different class in those days. They were often not just upper middle class but on the way to being aristocracy! Like the officers in the British Guards' regiments, it was just the done thing to recruit them from the upper classes. "Farquhar Finlay" would arrive at the Scottish regiment for three years just to get the badge because his old Uncle Hamish had been the general in the "thin red line" during the Boer War – and perhaps he came to the regiment from a school such as Gordonstoun, the famous boarding school in Moray, Scotland, or some other good public school where members of the royal family might have studied.

I know that is a stereotype, but it was how we thought then. So to become an officer from the ranks at that time was quite tricky. I didn't come from that sort of stock. My dad was a working-class Glaswegian and my mum came from a similar background. My view of officers was deeply coloured by all this and I didn't really know if I would make the transition to commissioned status that well – but I was surprised to discover that my superiors were not looking at my social suitability; they were looking at my leadership potential. I thought about it for a few days and made the mistake of confiding in one or two of my mates. I was abused by some of the guys for even thinking about becoming an officer, so after that day I didn't talk to any of the lads, but I told the regiment that I was willing to go forward for a commission if they felt it would be right.

I knew that I had crossed the line and that there would be no way back to my old pals, but I also felt an inward excitement at what might lie ahead. It was as if an undreamed-of new world was opening up in front of me. I soon found myself on a plane back to Scotland in order to attend a very important course known as the Pre-Royal Commissioning Board (Pre-RCB), once again at Glencorse Barracks. This time I found myself eating my meals in the officers' mess. I had not told the guys back at Minden that I was going on the Pre-RCB and I felt really quite guilty sitting there among all those toffs!

Before the three-day process of the Pre-RCB began I went home to see my parents. They were delighted to hear my news, of course, and insisted on going out to buy me a blazer with silver buttons on the front and a pair of corduroy trousers. I was now looking like a real "Rupert", as we called the younger officers. So, kitted out by Moss Bros, I went into the barracks to go through the selection process. The instructors who were in charge were the same guys who had taught me when I was at Glencorse the first time round. They were really pleased to see me and thought that it was great to have one of their own boys going through the course. I passed Pre-RCB and briefly went back to my regiment in Germany.

Unfortunately, by now word had got out that I was heading for a commission and things had changed completely. I wasn't in the circle any more and I remember it being quite a lonely time for me, but I understood how the guys ticked so I didn't hold it against them. I realized that I would have been just the same myself with one of them, as it was just the way we were trained and taught. There was a kind of understanding that you just did not betray your mates and go over to what they regarded as "the other side". So I was lonely and was glad to leave in the end for the next step in this process. I got sent to Beaconsfield for the Potential Officer Development Course (PODC) and this is where I first met Bev, who would later become my wife.

11

BEACONSFIELD AND BEV

Beaconsfield is a quintessentially picturesque English village in Buckinghamshire and the camp was very much designed in the same sort of style. It was known as Wilton Park, which does not even sound like an army barracks, and at its centre was a beautiful village green containing a cricket pitch and its very own pavilion. I had arrived there straight from a crazy and violent infantry environment and found myself suddenly immersed in "middle England", with its cricket matches and traditional "Pimms o'clock"! Yet, in spite of the huge cultural awakening I was going through, I felt that I was in a good place.

On the first day in Beaconsfield I found myself being shown into a cavernous theatre-style hall designed for the officer cadets and laid out with tables. Here we would be able to mingle, socialize, and learn. As I walked nervously through the doorway with its draping curtains it all seemed so civilized and a world away from the savagery I had experienced at Minden. I heard the gentle sounds of classical music being played in the background – Vivaldi's *Four Seasons*, I think. All around the room were placed writing desks in dark wood, perhaps mahogany or seasoned oak, with green-leather reading sections set into the top. On these desks were arranged the day's broadsheet newspapers, with titles such as the *Financial Times* and the *Daily Telegraph*. Until then it had always been the *Sun*, the *Daily Mirror*, or any of the other red-top tabloids for me, so I was intrigued.

I looked around at the motley crew of candidates for officership that had been gathered in that place and, from the look of them, I guessed that most had come from the ranks. We were all from different regiments and it was a real revelation to me that there were women as well as men. My experience of the army so far had been very much male-dominated and we did not have any women at the camps that I had been in. Previously the only female interest I had had was outside camp, but not a lot of it had been particularly savoury, as you can imagine. So far I had been immersed in quite a seedy world with regard to the opposite sex, and those were formative years for me for all the wrong reasons.

Anyhow, here at Beaconsfield women were in the same common room as me and in uniform, so I was quite shocked. Nervously, we sat down and officers from the Army Education Corps, mainly majors through to colonels, came in to introduce themselves as our teachers and instructors for the next few months. My time in Beaconsfield remains in my memory as one of the best six months of my life. It covered the summer of 1990, including the World Cup football competition famous for England's poor performance and "Gazza's tears", and the sun shone all the way through. I realize it probably didn't, but it just seemed that way to me. It was like being at one big holiday party after the extreme situation I had been used to where everyone was fighting and brawling on a Friday night.

I first saw Bev at Beaconsfield when I went over to the central stores to collect some bits of kit that I would need for my course. She was then a full corporal herself and was working in the stores. I liked what I saw and made a mental note to look her up some time. It would not be long before our paths crossed again.

As far as the socializing side of the course went, we had quite a good time. At first everything was civilized and a whole new experience for me – sipping different kinds of wine or enjoying gin and tonics – and as a result of this we got to meet the staff of the camp regularly on a social footing. Soon we were starting to let our hair down a bit. Each Thursday evening we held what was called the "NAAFI Bop", a disco where the drinks flowed freely and people from all parts of the camp would come together for a good time. Life in the military can be quite hedonistic. At that time there was a lot of sleeping around, even among married men and women and engaged people. Wherever alcohol was easily available, as it was at Beaconsfield, there was some of that going on.

One Thursday there was a themed dress night and the ladies were all done up in Roman togas. Bev was there and she was wrapped around with white towels or a sheet and the sight was quite interesting – well, it got me interested anyway. We'd had a few beers by then and were dancing, and while we gyrated around with me feeling increasingly drawn to her despite her apparent obliviousness to my pathetic attempts at clever dance moves, we began to move closer to each other. Finally she was right there in front of me and I was smitten. I pulled her towards me and kissed her right there among all the other dancers. For a few amazing seconds I was unaware of everyone else. When we pulled apart we just carried on dancing and that was it for the time being, but I was really quite struck with her in a way that I had not been with anyone before.

After that we didn't really meet again for a few weeks, and then we bumped into one another at the NAAFI bar. We downed a couple of beers and she invited me over to her block for a cup of tea. We lived in separate blocks then, of course, the males and the females, so I went and she made me a cup of tea and I stayed the night with her. We didn't do anything sexually that night (which was strange for military life); we spent most of the time just chatting and enjoying each other's company.

Following that Bev got ill with flu and I started to go over to her block while she was poorly just to see how she was and if there was anything I could get her. I was a bit worried about the fact that she had been in a relationship with another guy and still kept his photograph beside her bed. I found that probably for the first time in my life I was feeling a jealous about a girl. I really wanted to know whether this other guy was important to her and if I had any chance of taking his place. Then, one night while she was still unwell, as I was leaving the room I turned round and asked, "Hey, you don't mind if I kiss you again, do you?" Well she didn't and I did, and that was the point when it all changed, and when she got better and we held the NAAFI Bop again we were there as an item. And I caught the flu!

Looking back at that early stage, I can see now that the relationship was pretty much built on lust and sex. It was quite intense and we got to know each other really well, and I fell in love with Bev. This was the first time I had experienced a serious relationship. Bev had known a couple of guys but I had had no long-term relationships, so the feelings that I was experiencing then were brand new to me. Most of my encounters with the opposite sex had been one-night stands: as a soldier you don't generally have time to develop more meaningful relationships, and to be honest it is sometimes discouraged by the army. I was to discover this fact personally as our relationship intensified to the point at which we decided to get married – despite the fact that I was still training to be an officer. So we were wary of this once we knew we were getting serious.

There was another complicating factor. Bev was an NCO and I was earmarked to become an officer, and marriage between officers and other ranks was definitely frowned upon at that time. So, perhaps for the first time in my army career, I was behaving in a way that the military authorities would not be happy about. But I could not help myself.

Wilton Park was also a well-known training centre for other professional people who needed to sharpen up their social manners, etiquette, and elocution. Martin Bell the white-suited journalist was there, and John Suchet, later of ITN, was also around. I was singled out for elocution, of course, because of my strong Glaswegian accent. I was not happy about that, because in a sense it reinforced my feelings of inferiority, but one of my tutors, Captain Jill Mansour, worked really hard on my behalf and was a great influence on me.

Alongside us there was also the Army School for Foreign Languages, so we had Arab students who were learning English, among them the Sultan of Oman's son, and some members of the Saudi royal family. Members of the British diplomatic community also went to Wilton Park to brush up on their foreign languages and cultures. Even elite forces like the SAS were there, but although you would see them around the camp they would never socialize with anyone. We had to learn how to communicate properly and develop our presentation skills. I did not realize then that this was preparing me for what life would bring much later on, but at that stage I bristled a little under the weight of all this seemingly useless information. I had joined the army to become a fighter, and all this social and cultural stuff was way ahead of me. My broad Glaswegian accent simply would not do for a life of advancement through the hallowed ranks as an officer in the British Army.

12

ROWALLAN COMPANY AT SANDHURST

Following the Potential Officer Course at Beaconsfield we went forward for the Commissioning Board, which consisted of a three-day selection course. At this stage those of us who had come up from the ranks were going to be mixed in with civilians who had come from university or the world of business and who wanted to become army officers. The leaders gave us each a number and made us wear it printed on a coloured bib. It was like being back in school.

We were put into different groups and given a command task similar to many corporate or youth-orientated initiative tests. The instructors would say, "There's a barrel, there's a rope, and there's a plank of wood. You've got to get from here to there with your entire group without touching the ground." I was fine at that sort of thing after all my time in the ranks. Then they would form us into discussion groups to have debates about current affairs and topical issues of that time. Occasionally they would throw in a question designed to find out whether we were reading the right newspapers. I think this was when an interest in and fascination with news and current affairs was awakened within me, which continues to this day.

The Board wanted to prove that each candidate had a broad spectrum of interest in what was going on in the world. We also sat written exams, mostly trying to plan military-style operations. A map would be pinned on the board and we would be told that we were heading to find lost treasure; however, there would be a bomb going off and we would have to get our team there and back safely, calculating times, distances, and tactics. Finally there was the main interview, with each candidate facing a fearsome group of instructors and senior staff officers.

Then, for me, it was off back to Beaconsfield, and two days later I was summoned to the education centre at Wilton Park for the Board's results. I was really nervous by then because I knew that many people failed the Commissioning Board. As I entered the centre everything was set out very formally. I was called Mr Gilvear now, as I had left behind my rank as an NCO and become an officer cadet. There were about six of us from Beaconsfield waiting for news, so there was a bit of a queue to use the only telephone available. We were told to ring a certain number in order to find out how we had done. I went in second after Tom Murphy, my friend from the Fusiliers. He was a great lad from Stevenage and a gifted boxer, who did not look the part but turned out to be an excellent officer. He phoned first and was told "Pass via Rowallan Company", so he came out quite relieved. I went in after Tom and was told the same thing.

I too was relieved but I knew that the eleven-week Rowallan Company course would be a tough one. It had a reputation for being a horrendous course and at that time was rated as the third hardest behind the Royal Marines selection course and P Company, but as I had already done the latter I felt reasonably confident. Little did I know how wrong I was.

Rowallan Company at the Royal Military Academy, Sandhurst (RMAS) was named after an aristocrat called Lord Rowallan, who was Commandant of the Highland Fieldcraft Training Centre (HFTC) during the Second World War. It had been set up in 1943 for the purpose of developing leadership qualities in servicemen who had been graded "NY" (Not Yet) by the War Office Selection Boards looking for potential officers, at a time when the army was about to require a large number of junior officers to fight in Europe. Rowallan Company itself was established at Sandhurst in 1977 to address the high failure rate (70 per cent) of officer cadets on the Commissioning Boards at that time. The course was based on the training model developed in the 1940s by Lord Rowallan, who was consulted about the establishment of the Company.

Since 1977, fifty-three courses had been completed in all, and, of the 2,900 cadets who started those courses, 65 per cent were successful. Of the successful Rowallan cadets, 92 per cent did well in their subsequent officer training and many of them reached high rank in the service. The Company was disbanded for financial reasons in 2002 but has been succeeded by a new course called "the Sandhurst Development Course", which is shorter and involves smaller numbers.

Rowallan Company's ethos of punishing failure and rewarding success, alongside total uncertainty, was supposed to be tremendously motivating for cadets, and its philosophy – "Develop character first and military leadership will follow" – may have worked for some, but it nearly destroyed me.

In Rowallan Company we were treated like dogs. I had

been through the Glencorse infantry training school after having gone through Harrogate with its harsh "Junior Brecon" regime, and had also done P Company, but nothing prepared me for the horrors of Rowallan Company. Maybe by that stage my drinking and my arrogance had begun to take a serious toll on me, but, despite all that I had endured up to that point in the military, this harsh preparation programme at Sandhurst nearly destroyed me physically and mentally. It broke me in a way that I had never experienced before.

I was unprepared, for instance, for the fact the instructors starved us and made us undertake intense physical training on practically a few grains of rice. I was treated worse there than I had been as a boy soldier, and it was a real shock to me. Through my mind went thoughts like, "Hang on – this is supposed to be to make me into an officer and a gentleman! How can this be?" My visions of tea in china cups and an ironed copy of a broadsheet newspaper at breakfast were rudely shattered. During those dreadful eleven weeks in Rowallan Company they would take us to the cookhouse for "meal parade" whether it was breakfast, dinner, or tea, and they would give us only just enough time for the first person to finish eating before yelling at us and forcing us back out again. If you were last in the queue, once that first person had finished you were gone before you had even sat down. We used to have to shove bread or cornflakes or any food we could get hold of into our mouths as we dropped our trays.

From there they used to take us on a 5-mile (8 km) run, and if we didn't do that well enough to match their high demands we were marched to a block in Old College at Sandhurst outside which we had what was again called the Mean Machine; in civilian terms it was basically a climbing frame but it consisted of bars that we were made to hang from for what seemed like ages. The staff would keep us there interminably. I remember hanging there exhausted, screaming in agony, starving hungry, and losing weight. I had never been treated like this before in my entire career. Our hunger drove us to forage for anything we could eat while on exercises, digging up raw vegetables with our bare hands and grabbing anything that looked vaguely edible. It was like being a prisoner of war in a really harsh enemy regime.

During this time we were given weekend leave and Bev said that she could not believe the shape of me when I arrived at Beaconsfield, where she was still based. I was white and gaunt like a prison camp inmate, and she wondered what they had done to me. Another guy on the course with me, who also had a girlfriend at Beaconsfield, went with me to the pub to have a quick pint while we were waiting for the girls to finish work. We couldn't finish the pints we ordered. After I had drunk about half of mine I went outside and was violently sick. I just couldn't keep anything down.

The previous week we'd been on an exercise right up to the Friday morning. We had time for a brief shower and got out of camp on that Friday afternoon, travelling straight on to Beaconsfield, and it was only then that we realized how tired we were. It just hit us like a wall, and we slept for most of the weekend. The speed marches we did at Rowallan Company were usually undertaken in appalling weather, as once again we were doing it as part of a January intake – as had been the case right from the start of my time in the forces. In that week before my leave we had been trudging for days and had covered miles on end, approximately 32 (51.5 km) per day, in fact. Our feet were in pieces and we were not allowed to stop except for food. However, upon stopping to eat we were so tired that when we sat down and got out our meagre rations we would nod off to sleep while eating them.

I know now that this was actually a sign not just of tiredness, but, in those freezing conditions of sleet and snow, of the fact that hypothermia was setting in. Once I found that I was nodding off while I was actually marching, which probably meant that hypothermia was disrupting my self-awareness. In other words, I didn't really know where I was or what I was doing. As I began to lose it on that march one of my mates called out to me, "Come on, Bill, keep going. Not long now, mate!" I don't really know how the civilians on the course coped with all this: I suppose it was really hard on them too but they had no previous experience of the army to measure it against so they probably thought this was the norm. But I knew that this was extreme, so it might actually have been easier mentally for them than for me.

As the Easter of 1991 approached I was ready to quit, but I knew that I had to buckle down and carry on because there was no way that I wanted to go through all that again. I could hardly believe it when I was told that I had passed and would be going on within Sandhurst and starting the main Commissioning Course.

13

THE WHITE HOUSE AT SANDHURST

As I approached my new home, from the outside it looked just like the American president's White House. Its light Regency-style exterior viewed across manicured lawns guarded by Victorian cannons encompassed by chain-link fences was imposing enough. As I entered the sacred porch, however, I was immediately struck by the strong smell of disinfectant and polish. Gone was the usual mixture of old sweat, stale cigarettes, and socks which had adorned most of my previous barracks postings like the odour of a meat market in the early morning before the start of trade. The order and state of preparedness in this place scared even me. I knew I had arrived at a special place in the life of the British Army.

The Royal Military Academy Sandhurst (RMAS), commonly known simply as Sandhurst, is located in the town of that name in Berkshire, England. The Academy's stated aim is to be "the national centre of excellence for leadership". In a television documentary in 2011 about the place I saw the new intake of officer cadets assemble in the chapel, just as I had done, at the start of their Commissioning Course. Their officer commanding was addressing them, and he challenged them with the definition of leadership given by Field Marshal Lord Montgomery of El Alamein. He said, "Leadership is that capacity and the will to rally men and women to a common purpose and the character which will inspire confidence. Such leadership must be based on a moral authority and it must be based on the truth."

That statement remains with me today as a real source of inspiration, but back then I don't think I had the foggiest idea about "moral authority" or "truth", and my character was pretty well shot to pieces. I was bruised after my time in Rowallan Company and sorry to be back at stage one in yet another training situation. My life was beginning to lose its focus just at the time when we were all being challenged to gain one.

All British Army officers, as well as many from elsewhere in the world, are trained at Sandhurst. The main Commissioning Courses start in January, May, and September of each year, so I joined the May entry. The training is split up into three terms, each lasting fourteen weeks, and on each course cadets are put into one of three companies. There can be as many as ten companies within the RMAS at any one time, each commanded by a major and named after a famous battle in which the British Army has fought. The course lasts forty-four weeks and must be successfully completed by all who want to qualify as British regular army officers before they receive their commission.

Training at Sandhurst covers military, practical, and academic subjects and, while it is mentally and physically demanding, there's also time set aside for sport and adventure training. The place is a cross between a very elegant English stately home and an army barracks. Life in the institution is how I imagine public school to be. In the documentary, someone called it "Hogwarts with guns!" Each morning at five we would be shaken awake and expected to be on parade in our uniform for the day, standing to attention in the corridor, within thirty minutes. We were yelled and sworn at by the staff but it was all very mild compared with Rowallan Company and in many ways I enjoyed it, although most of the other guys on the Commissioning Course appeared to me to be real "Ruperts" – the name we gave to posh officers in the Argylls. It's a proud day, though, for officer cadets going into the regular army when they finally march up the steps of Old College to be commissioned as officers at the end of the prestigious Sovereign's Parade. When my turn eventually came, Prince Michael of Kent was taking the royal salute and it was both a relief and a really special moment for me and for my family once again. Little did they know how close I was to throwing the whole thing away.

One of my bones of contention with the military at this time was my relationship with Bev. Despite my being so busy at Old College preparing for the life of an officer and drinking very heavily whenever we were allowed leave, I asked Bev to marry me.

The army definitely would not have approved. I was preparing to become a newly minted officer, known as a subaltern. In some regiments they would not take a young trainee officer if they were in a serious relationship because the regiment preferred their junior officers to experience life in the officers' mess as singles. They also liked to use young officers, second lieutenants or lieutenants, to do all the unwanted jobs such as duty officer of the day and such like. So they didn't like you having a commitment to a woman if you were male.

Mind you, they did like you to be able to invite a woman along when you needed an escort for the Mess Ball, but they didn't approve of long-term relationships interfering with army life.

My decision to marry Bev thus did not sit well with my superiors, but in my arrogance I felt that I could not care less. In the event the whole plan for us to marry became a nightmare for Bev, with me pulling out at the last minute, causing real outrage among family members on both sides and the cancellation of an expensive wedding. A few weeks later I begged Bev to give me another chance and we did get married, in the November of my year at Sandhurst, in a very low-key civil ceremony. But by this stage I was in deep trouble, not just with the military but in my head. I was drinking seriously and dangerously whenever I could manage to do it without jeopardizing my studies. Up to then drinking had been a social thing and I hadn't thought I had a problem, but it was at this point that I started to drink to escape from myself and my memories. All of a sudden alcohol became medicine for me, and from that moment on I drank to try to ease all my pain. It was also at this point that the barrier to facing myself and my past that the military had provided began to crumble and I started to look seriously at civilian life.

After the course at Sandhurst I was sent as an acting second lieutenant over Christmas and the early part of the New Year to the Regimental History Office of the Highland Fusiliers in Glasgow. This allowed me to experience the atmosphere in the officers' mess as well as see something of civilian life as I travelled to and from the office in Sauchiehall Street.

During this time of relative ease after all the rigours of army life, I started to envy the people who worked in the offices around me. Their lives seemed so easy compared with mine, and it seemed to me that they enjoyed tremendous freedom as well as greater financial rewards. In my heart the brutality of Rowallan Company was festering. Taken together with the feelings I now had for Bev, and an increasing sense that the army had treated me badly, it had brought me to a fork in the road. Some of the friends I had made in the military were now leaving, saying that there were rich pickings to be made by ex-soldiers in the close protection business. To be honest, I would probably have believed them even if they had told me the streets were paved with gold. In my increasingly desperate lifestyle and my arrogance, I wondered whether the time was maybe coming for me to try to find a life outside the military. My downward spiral was winding ever more tightly. Soon it would spin me completely out of control. Well, out of *my* control, anyway.

14

TO WED OR NOT TO WED?

I was head over heels in love with Bev as my time in the army drew to a close, but it wasn't a normal relationship. That was my fault, really, as I was quite insecure because of my increasing drinking and the fallout from the trauma of going through Rowallan Company and starting my training all over again. In addition to all that I was paranoid that she might be sleeping with someone else, as often happened in the military. Not that she would have done, of course, but, because of my own behaviour and all that I had seen around me over the years, these thoughts were there in the back of my mind. I really didn't want to lose her.

So we made plans to marry during a leave break that was coming up in my Sandhurst course. It was all arranged, mainly by Bev, to be the wedding every girl would want to have. Loads of guests were invited, bridesmaids were chosen and kitted out with their dresses, and the church plus the vicar were booked. Everything was set up including the flowers and even a Rolls Royce to take us from the church to the big posh reception, and then I got cold feet, and with only a week to go I called the wedding off. It was horrendously thoughtless of me to do that, but I was in such a state of fear and uncertainty.

Despite being really messed up in my thinking I knew straight away that I had let Bev and everyone else down very badly. Her parents were furious, and mine were none too impressed either. Nursing a hangover, I went home to Scotland still very much part of the Sandhurst scene, and basically I got drunk from the time that I got home, much to my parents' displeasure, but I just did not care any more.

Bev was devastated, of course, and she showed it! I don't blame her, but we had a robust kind of relationship in which we partied hard and argued hard. When I plucked up the courage to tell her face to face that the wedding was off she went ballistic. After that she went to stay with her sister in Nottingham, where her brother-in-law was a staff sergeant in the Royal Engineers.

One night I phoned Bev and found, unsurprisingly, that she felt crushed by what I had done. I was so affected by the phone call and how I had hurt her by calling off the wedding and ruining her dream day that I got a taxi from Sauchiehall Street in Glasgow all the way to Nottingham! The black cab cost me about three hundred pounds, which was a horrendous amount, but I was so drunk and so desperate to see her again that it didn't register. I did not tell my parents what had happened or where I was going. I just took off from Glasgow like a thief in the night, and it wasn't till I arrived in Nottingham the next day that I contacted Mum and Dad. As you can imagine, my mum was really worried about me and my dad went mad.

During this whole period I was almost out of my head with alcohol. My ankle was giving me a lot of pain all the time, as was my back, and this was interfering with my physical activities in the military. The mental and emotional pain of my childhood was also resurfacing at this time as the security blanket of the army began to fall away. The prospect of leaving the safe familiarity of the forces, together with apprehension about being married and yet the strong fear of losing Bev for ever, meant that my emotions were becoming increasingly raw; my life seemed to be falling apart and I felt more and more exposed. Drink became my treatment method of choice for all these ills, and Bev and those around me were paying the price for it. Sadly, things were about to get much worse.

Once the waters had settled a bit over the cancelled wedding, Bev and I decided to give it another go. This time we were married at a register office in Wales in November with very few guests there at all. It was not what Bev had dreamed of, but at least we were wed and could start facing life together. None of my family came to the ceremony and I knew that once again I had let them down badly. With all that was going on in my life, my only solace was to be found either in Bev's arms or at the bottom of a bottle, or both. When my assignment with the Royal Highland Fusiliers came to an end Bev drove me down to Sandhurst again so that I could finalize details of my commission at New College. I had an interview with an ancient officer who was Colonel of the Regiment, a formal position usually given to a retired general, and that seemed to go quite well.

After this I was called into the office of a Major Jones, of the Welsh Guards. I was standing ramrod straight to attention in his room. He scowled at me and said, "What's happening to you, Mr Gilvear?"

I said, "My head's gone, Sir; it's just gone!"

"Whatever do you mean, lad?"

"Well, I don't know what I'm doing and my life is just a mess." I told him then that I would be bad news for the army. I had gone from being a great soldier to a bad one and the whole façade of my drivenness had crumbled.

He looked at me with a degree of pity mixed with frustration and said, "Mr Gilvear, you have trained all this time to become an officer and a gentleman and now you have got to think about this seriously, because your commission is there just waiting for you if you want it."

"I know, Sir, thank you." I had done my stuff with the Highland Fusiliers and enjoyed it. Living as an officer at Oakington Barracks in Cambridgeshire where they were based at that time had been fun, as had the hectic social scene in Glasgow. But I knew myself well enough to realize that the game was up, although I had not told Bev. Major Jones said that I would have to see the medical officer (MO) the following Monday, so I went home to Wales for the weekend. Bev's dad drove me from Wales to Sandhurst to see the doctor – a meeting at which I knew a final decision about my future would have to be made. When I saw the MO he realized that I had enough physical problems to qualify for a medical discharge if I wanted one.

Even then the choice was still mine. I didn't have the courage to tell Bev that at the time, because I knew that she had given up her army career so that I could pursue becoming an officer. So I lied and told her that I was getting medically discharged against my will. Nowadays that might indeed be the case, because there would be no option, but at that time I could have decided just to keep on despite the pain and discomfort.

The fact that some of the guys in my old units had told me that there was big money to be made on the outside in close protection – becoming a bodyguard to the rich and famous – meant that this was now a possibility in the back of my mind. Anyhow, I made my decision to go, and that was it. I was given six months' resettlement pay and by June 1992 I was a civilian again.

15

WELCOME TO THE CELEBRITY LIFESTYLE!

I had to pinch myself to be sure this was not a dream. I really was sitting on a black leather settee in London's Hard Rock Café at 2 a.m. chatting alone with the famous star of stage and silver screen, Robert Downey, Jr. Even though he was not yet as well known as he would later become, he was already evolving into one of the most respected actors in Hollywood, with an amazing list of credits to his name. In 1992, Downey received an Academy Award nomination and won the British Academy Film and Television Award (BAFTA) for best actor because of his performance in the title role of the movie *Chaplin*. So why was this famous face from the world of film bothering to spend time in the early hours telling the likes of me his life story?

He wasn't the only celebrity to do so, mind you. By then I had become part of the close protection business I had heard about, acting as a bodyguard to the stars and famous bands of the time. Most of our work involved keeping the fans and the paparazzi away from our clients, and so we spent a lot of quality time in close proximity to some very well-known people. Gradually some of them came to put their trust in us and we would sometimes find ourselves on the inside track into their emotional and private lives.

I was hardly the right person to advise anybody about those subjects just then, as my own emotional life was in a real mess, but I could identify with Downey as he poured out his fevered concerns over a glass of whisky and after a line or two of cocaine. As is clear from Martin Howden's biography of the actor,[7] Robert Downey was really messed up by drink and drugs at that point in his career and I was well on my way to joining him, despite – or maybe because of – my newfound intimacy with the rich and famous.

As soon as I had made the decision to leave the army I regretted it. From Sandhurst with all its pomp, ceremony, and order I travelled reluctantly back to Wales to move in with Bev at her parents' house, squashing together in her old bedroom. The period leading up to this had been marked by increasing disillusionment with my life, the army, and the world in general. I suppose that through my relationship with Bev and her parents I was starting to face problems that I had run away from for years.

Many children rebel while they are still at home. My rebellion only really took off at this point in my life, as the restraining influence of the boundaries set by the military was suddenly removed. I was exposed to the world in a serious way for the first time, and although I was married and with Bev I felt pretty much on my own without the discipline of military life to sustain me. My mind was just boiling over with sadness, anger, and frustration at the way things had turned out for me. I would sit with Bev and pour out my sorrows to her but it was hard for her to listen to it all. I remember,

---

7   Martin Howden, *Robert Downey Jr: The Biography* (John Blake Publishing, London, 2010), p. 129.

in particular, sitting there on the bed in her room one night just crying real hot tears while holding a half-empty bottle of wine, wondering what I had done to deserve this and what my life had become.

Obviously it was hard for Bev's parents to have this melancholy drunk around the house and there were occasionally what seemed to be major disputes with her mum and dad, but they were usually over something trivial that had been blown out of all proportion. I was just so angry, and we knew that we needed our own space.

In time we made the move to Sidcup in Kent and I started working in the personal security field with a top arts security company. This was headed up by a guy called Jerry Judge, who is still active in the world of close protection today and is widely respected for his work. Jerry himself was a real Irish character from Dublin and one of his early claims to fame in the UK was being the first "Yorkie" man in the TV adverts for the chocolate bar of that name. He was the male model shown driving the truck with his own Yorkie bar and, a bit of a contradiction really, he had shining white teeth.

Jerry was also very handy with his fists. He was large, fearless, and handsome and like many a great Irishman he was a tremendous communicator, with a wicked sense of humour. He was destined to play a significant role in my life. Perhaps once again, as with the sergeant majors in my past, he became a kind of father figure to me at a time when I was deeply unhappy.

Jerry and another man called Alf Weaver had started in the security trade by looking after the band U2. Alf was then in his sixties and had been in the music industry for a long time, having looked after the Monkees and for a little while even the Beatles. He had been tour manager and head of security for the rock group Status Quo, and he and Jerry got together to form an alliance that went on to become a very successful security company for the film and music industry. They were particularly known for offering much more than just close protection. Each celebrity was offered a service that was, in effect, their own personal concierge. Their employees were trained in communication, protection, and all that was required to pamper and take care of the client.

I heard about their outfit from a mate in the army and thought there might be something in it for me. We moved to London and I approached Jerry for a job. At first I think Alf was a bit wary of this diminutive Scotsman with attitude, but the army background always helped and Jerry said he would give me a try. I started working with them predominantly in the London area, looking after security in clubs called Planet Hollywood and the Hard Rock Café, which at that time were frequented by a lot of celebrities. Planet Hollywood had grown out of the Hard Rock Café idea with a similar atmosphere, seeking the endorsement of the stars in order to make the outlets attractive and successful. The club in Coventry Street near Piccadilly Circus had just opened and planned a big jamboree to celebrate, with famous names such as Kevin Costner, Arnold Schwarzenegger, and Sylvester Stallone in attendance.

It really was just like Hollywood in London, and while the big launch was going on my job was mainly guarding the doors to keep photographers out and to make sure that nobody went in or out except those who should have done. The atmosphere was incredible and Robert Earl, who owned Planet Hollywood and the Hard Rock Café together with the Orlando Magic basketball team, said that he liked what he saw of me. It was a kind of who's who of show business and I had passed the test as someone to be trusted in that environment; Jerry then offered me more work.

16

BIG BREAKFAST **BIRTHDAY BASH**

The next job would also be a kind of test and involved the popular Channel 4 television programme *Big Breakfast*, famous for conducting interviews in a huge double bed. Presenters Chris Evans, Gaby Roslin, and Ulrika Jonsson were prominent in the programme and they planned to celebrate its first anniversary in style. The *Big Breakfast* Birthday Party bash was to be held at the Royal Horticultural Society buildings in London, one of the most elegant and stylish venues in the capital, and when Jerry phoned he said, "If you can get up there we will have another look to see how you get on."

The venue had been set up to echo the *Big Breakfast* theme, including a huge four-poster bed on which some of the celebrities were sprawled drinking champagne even as I arrived. I explored a bit and found that there were bars all around to both left and right, at which young waiters were deftly tossing bottles up in the air and juggling with glasses and ice cubes to produce exotic cocktails. Upstairs on a mezzanine area there was a dance floor with a DJ providing music that thumped and bumped like a primitive call to war. That was not the only dancing area, though, because through a curtain to the side of the big bed there was another place already heaving with guests. There were a lot of very drunk people around and a good deal of smooching and intimate dancing going on.

I thought the atmosphere was fantastic – quite jovial, really – and my job was to look after the celebrities and make sure that they had all that they needed. I was not a bouncer, as they were already in place, but I was to supervise the guest list and just make sure that there was no one there who should not be. The occasion had been arranged by Matthew Freud (great-grandson of the famous Sigmund and son of the late writer and humorist Sir Clement Freud), who runs a highly successful PR company organizing special events for the stars. He was someone I was destined to get to know very well in time, but this was my first encounter with a big event put on by him. Jerry was there too, so he introduced me to one or two of the key players, including Matthew, and then just sent me off on my own to mingle.

So here I was on my second job, little Billy Gilvear, moving among these famous guests just as they had taught us at Beaconsfield, greeting them like long-lost friends. I would sidle up to them and coo in their ear, "Hello! How lovely to see you. Do you have all that you need?" or maybe, "Are you having a lovely time? Is there anything else I can get for you?"

Mind you, there was a limit to how far that familiarity could go. During that memorable evening one of the guys on the security team forgot his place and tried to become one of the celebrities. This was a big no-no in the business. He began not only to engage them in conversation but to drink with them too, and by the end of the night he was on the dance floor with some of the birthday guests. I was learning the rules of this new job fast as I observed the anger of his colleagues. He lost his job that night, though typically of Jerry and Alf it was done in such a way that the guests would not have known, but as a result I found myself being pushed up the chain of command. My army training just took over, giving me an awareness of my surroundings and the flexibility to do whatever needed to be done.

Once we had our rogue security man out of the way, we were left with a lot of celebrities in varying degrees of incapacity who needed help to get home. I spent a lot of time late that night carrying semiconscious guests to their cars. As the party wore on into the early hours I had the dubious pleasure of carrying out an infamous "A" list lady actor and finding myself the object of her amorous advances! The job had indeed become quite personal and physical but this was going far beyond anything that I had expected. I really wanted to please Jerry, who was already becoming that much-sought-after father figure to me, and I knew he was watching me that night, so I just did my job and delivered my tipsy charge to her limousine.

Jerry saw this and started to take a keen interest in this wiry, hyped-up little Scotsman. Some of the other guys in the team who had been with him for a while noticed this and were a bit concerned, but he told me, "You know, Billy, you're a fun guy and we're going to have to watch this fun because we don't want you turning out like the rogue security man we've just carried out tonight! But you'll do, my son, if you're careful."

I was OK with that, as it was still early in my employment. It gave me a warm feeling inside to hear those words from a guy like Jerry, who was so respected by all, and I felt that perhaps I had at last come home to where I was meant to be. Sadly, I was wrong, and it would be mostly downhill from that point on. This was not home; this was tinsel town.

17

LIFE IN THE CITY

That night Jerry gave me a permanent job, assigning me to take care of Planet Hollywood and to work in the Hard Rock Café in nearby Old Park Lane. They were both restaurants/ bar bistros that some described as "the celebrities' upmarket burger bars". Planet Hollywood also contained a private cinema, so, for example, on Sunday mornings celebrities would turn up with their kids and sit them down in front of a movie. Brian May of the band Queen and his partner (now wife), Anita Dobson, from the BBC television show *EastEnders*, used to come in with their kids and ask me to settle them in front of the screen while they had a drink and a bite to eat. I would make sure they were OK and then keep the place free of photographers or nosey parkers. May, a founding member of Queen, was a world-renowned guitarist and songwriter even then, with a string of London West End theatre successes to his name, so the press would have loved to get a snap of him with his family.

Boris Becker was another frequent visitor to Planet Hollywood, especially since we held an annual Wimbledon jamboree there, when the doors were closed to the public so that the Wimbledon players could get together. I remember top names from the world of tennis coming in and asking me to keep the press off their tails and giving me some extra cash if I made sure there were no pictures taken. Of course I did what I was asked to do, sometimes making myself a bit unpopular with the paparazzi, but ensuring that my relationship with Jerry and his clients was improving all the time.

Meanwhile, back at home, my relationship with Bev – who was now pregnant – was deteriorating just as fast. I was, after all, pretty much a nocturnal animal, leaving home in the late afternoon to train in the gym and spread my body out on a sunbed to boost my tan. Then I was off out until nearly daybreak. I slept in for most of the day, and, on the occasions when Bev and I did meet, the atmosphere between us was becoming tense. I also scanned the newspapers, cutting out any photos of myself in close company with the stars, while all the while the real star in my life was languishing alone at home. When Bev and I were arguing one day she told me that she saw me in the back garden sometimes when I was at home, prowling up and down like a caged tiger with a mobile phone stuck to my ear and yelling out to some unseen person at the other end. I really was hot-wired in those days.

Wimbledon fortnight was not the only time we closed these restaurants to the public so that famous acts could have the place all to themselves for private parties and celebrations, such as receiving an MTV award or such like. One night the blues band Aerosmith, once described as "America's greatest rock and roll band", were playing at the Wembley Arena and they came down after the main concert to the Hard Rock Café and played live on a mini stage in the restaurant.

It was more than a bit surreal, but there I was in the middle of it all. At first it had seemed like magic to me to be working in such close proximity to so many famous people, but the magic dust soon began to blow off. When the Premiership footballers came there would often be real mayhem. One night Tottenham, a leading London team, were in Planet Hollywood for their Christmas party. The event deteriorated into a mass food fight in which they started throwing onions at first, and then before you knew it every other food item they could get their hands on. It was pure carnage, and I was the one supposed to control this and make sure the other clients trying to have a quiet cocktail were happy too! It was a bizarre occasion, and just one among many.

Along with all this decadence and high-pressure living, we sometimes encountered characters from the world of glamour and modelling, who were really high maintenance. Legendary models would turn up and be very demanding and rude to all the staff, security included. Sometimes I would listen to them talking down to and snapping orders at people, and was amazed that nobody hit them! The real battle was keeping the cameras at bay as much as possible, especially in areas where they might be changing their clothes.

Once, during London Fashion Week, we were looking after the models at a time when Naomi Campbell was dating Adam Clayton from the band U2, and the press were all over them, with photographers everywhere. Naomi and Yasmin Le Bon, a British–Iranian supermodel of that era, were due to perform a show at the Natural History Museum and were trying to make an entrance unseen.

Adam arrived late in a chauffeur-driven limo and went round to the back door so as to slip in and see Naomi.

Jerry was with me on that job and spoke to me in his usual robust way.

"Don't you let those f****** paparazzi anywhere near him! If they do, give them some of this" – brandishing his fists like a prizefighter at a weigh-in. Jerry used profanities with a style and panache that I had never really come across before, even in the army, so this was nothing unusual, but it got my attention. His normal method of training was "Communicate – move – get away", so this was the first time I had heard him being so direct. I was at that back door wearing my earpiece, and just as I got the message that Adam was arriving, a particular photographer, who also turned out to be Irish like Jerry, was really pestering me, so I called out to Jerry for help. Behind the fire door I was protecting, which was slightly ajar, I knew that there was a host of fabulous supermodels, half naked! They would have made a great shot for a press photographer, so I needed some back-up. Jerry came storming in, grabbed the camera from the stroppy Irishman, and refused to give it back. While the pack was distracted I hustled Adam safely inside the door without revealing too much of the flesh of the multi-million pound harem inside. He removed the film from the camera and handed back the remains.

"Get out of here, you son of a b****!" he yelled at the protesting photographer, seizing me by the arm and dragging me off towards the front door, where, after straightening his tie and dusting down his suit, he was soon back glad-handing the celebs with not a sign of his exertion.

"Hello there. How are you doing? How's the family?" he mouthed with a huge smile, showing all his usual aplomb. What a man! What absolute madness! Yet this was my brave new world.

18

ON THE ROAD

When I started to work for Jerry the main band on the music scene were Take That, who had become a huge phenomenon all over the UK and Europe. Jerry's company was given the contract for looking after security for the band, and we all knew that this job would take us out of London and around the country on tour. So, from working in the clubs and looking after celebrities such as Wesley Snipes and Mel Gibson with his wife and children for a little while, my life now moved on to the road.

For me it was probably the right job but at the wrong time, because I was still seething with anger and frustration and I needed an outlet for that. The military with its controlled aggression and discipline had given me such an outlet, but all that was gone now, and unfortunately in this new field of work there was no moral framework to keep me on the right path. In fact, right at the core of it there was quite a rebellious attitude that was not exactly healthy for me in my low state of mind. Celebrity culture then as now encouraged self-expression through drink, drugs, and debauchery. Most of the people I met were anti-establishment and pretty much anti- anything sensible at all, really – especially such things as a military framework of service or self-discipline. So here I was, an angry young man at one of the most vulnerable times in my life, being submerged in a climate that applauds rebellion and encourages self-indulgence of all kinds.

My anger and frustration were also inflamed because I was still drinking heavily and was now being introduced to drugs for the first time in my life. The party drug ecstasy was plentiful at that point, particularly in London, and I started taking it from time to time, even offering it to others. Sadly, during that early period among the stars, I came into contact with cocaine as well. At first I was shocked to discover certain celebrities whom I would never have expected to be drug users doing so freely and openly. Soon any surprise was gone. Sometimes, as part of taking care of them, I used to have to stand outside the toilet door while they were doing their cocaine and other drugs. There were really crazy things going on behind locked doors that the press never got to publish, largely thanks to guys like me. I had encountered a free and easy attitude to morals and sex in the army, but that was nothing compared with life among the rich and famous.

Soon I was lulled into accepting this fantasy world as if it were normal. In the back of my mind I knew that it was wrong, but I was so struck by the lure of their riches and fame that I chose to hush any dissenting thoughts and to overlook the obvious insecurity and deep emptiness in these people. Soon even those thoughts disappeared as I was sucked ever more deeply down.

One story that didn't shock me, because I already knew how things had been for him as a lot had been published even at that early stage, was that of Robert Downey, Jr. I felt sad at his situation because deep down he was a nice guy. Unlike some of the clients he would sit with me and chat, whereas others took the view that the bodyguards were there just to offer a service by looking after them and keeping threats at bay, no more. For most of them the biggest threat they faced was from some screaming fan who wanted to get a chunk of their clothing or a kiss from them, so we weren't talking about diplomats whose lives were at risk or members of the royal family who really needed our protection. Nevertheless, they liked the fact that a security man would follow them around, fending off the crazies and making them appear important.

We were paid well for it too, so no complaint from me on that score, but Robert Downey, Jr was different. In the early hours of the morning, after a long day in the studio, he sought me out in the bar at Planet Hollywood. He beckoned me across to the lounge area where he was sitting, nursing his double whisky, and invited me to join him. I was happy to do so because my duties were light that night and I was intrigued to be in the company of someone I really rated highly. Once I sat down, he started mumbling and talking away and I realized that he was fairly drunk already. Anyhow, that night we laughed and chatted together and had a deep, meaningful conversation, no doubt well lubricated by the alcohol, but I was really moved by this guy and his story. I thought, "Wow, deep down beneath this drug-induced absolute carnage that is his life now, in and out of prison and all that, he is a sensitive bloke who's got a lot to offer." I felt a real empathy with him and a deep sorrow for his loss – and for my own.

19

TOURING AND TROUBLE

The contract to provide tour security for the top rock "boy band" Take That took me off around the UK, and indeed around Europe, with them. We took care of them, especially at their hotel, which is where most of our action took place. Getting them to and from concerts and gigs was fairly routine and extremely well planned, so there was not much opportunity for misbehaviour, but once they got back to their luxury hotel it was something different. These hotels were sometimes packed with girls known as "groupies", who either hung around the various places where they could catch a glimpse of their idols, or had planned ahead and booked themselves into the best hotel near the venue in the hope that the boys would stay there.

For this reason we were sometimes forced to book hotels quite a distance away from the place where the band was booked to play, but these girls were real fanatics, and they would find us wherever we went. Most of our work was trying to keep them from the band. They would do anything, including use physical violence, to get near them, and I had my eyes and face scratched on many an occasion. It was war!

Generally we would book an entire floor of a hotel so that we could set up a secure perimeter, but sometimes the girls would even proposition us with sexual favours if we would let them through. This was also the case with really attractive girls in their twenties, not just young teens, and even with the people working at the hotel. The room staff and others would get involved with the security guys so that they could find out where Gary Barlow was sleeping or in which bed Robbie Williams had been, just so that they could lie in it themselves, sometimes with a security man in tow! The band's manager emphasized to us that he did not want these girls to get to them, because their image at the time was that of a group of clean-cut young men on the music scene, poster boys who were featuring in *Smash Hits* magazine and so on, so he didn't want them to be besmirched by reports of womanizing.

Along with the band, of course, there were a large number of pop dancers, who were pretty fit and full of energy. They were sometimes staying inside the perimeter at the hotels, but they also had a lot of access to the boys and each other backstage, where it often became quite frisky, even while a gig was going on. All this was taking place in a kind of bubble of unreality, like one of those glass balls you shake to create artificial snow inside it. Within our little glass bubble on tour we were living this high-energy, high-impact life, far removed from the everyday realities most of us normally face, protected and cosseted so that our every whim was taken care of.

Being on the road is a very demanding and tiring experience for all concerned and it takes its toll on both individuals and families, and especially on marriages, as you can imagine. Mine was no exception. Fatigue was a main feature of this kind of security work, because when the band were working so were we, but when they were resting, we were still on duty to protect them. Each week we would have a day off, but we could not go far as they might still call on us at any point. It was reminiscent of the kind of weariness I used to know in the army, and it does undermine your resolve and your sense of what is good for you, or even of right and wrong.

While we were on duty we could not drink alcohol, and even on our days off we were careful not to overdo it, knowing we might be called back in. But the band took their down time very seriously and indulged fairly freely. As has been well publicized elsewhere, Robbie Williams was a kind of all-or-nothing person who went at life with a will. He was a great supporter of Port Vale Football Club too, and was friends with a number of the big names in the sport. As a result, men from the Premiership made regular calls at the hotel floor. At various times David James, goalkeeper for Liverpool and England, Robbie Fowler, Jamie Redknapp, and Steve McManaman all turned up for Robbie's parties. They liked Robbie because of his energy. Not only were Take That the guys to be seen with, but Robbie had a reputation for taking partying on to another level. He gave off this amazing buzz and always had such a presence about him, and he was a genuine and kind-hearted guy, so others were naturally attracted to him.

All this was way beyond the rules set down by their management, but we in security were in a dilemma. If Robbie jumped into a car and shot off we simply had no choice but to go with him. Thankfully, more recently, Robbie has managed to pull himself back from all that excess, and he has been off the booze for quite a few years. At that time, though, he was really heading for trouble (and for the break-up of the band), but I found him such a likeable bloke. I was beginning to go seriously downhill myself then, so I was not paying too much attention to all this. Not in the world of celebrity, of course, but in my own little circles I would say to people, "Follow me and we will really party! We'll go to another level here and get drunk, get drugs, whatever you want. If we're going to party, then let's party!"

Keeping a band out of the way of the press was often difficult. In one northern English city, band members that we were responsible for announced to us that they were going to a nightclub. Their manager was not at all happy, and nor were we, but there was little we could do. There was a very high risk that something bad would happen and the papers would be all over it. We warned the bar that they were coming and so the doormen knew what to expect, and prepared a VIP section for them.

Inevitably, there were guys in the club who were jealous, especially when their girls showed an obvious interest in these personalities. On this particular night a girl who was being eyed up by the band or their entourage was being mistreated by her boyfriend, and a band member saw it. He was not happy about it, and got involved, which was a nightmare for us. Fists began to fly and we hustled in to separate them and get the boys out. We disappeared into the night leaving the fight roaring like a log fire behind us. The band's manager was furious and scoured the papers the next day for the inevitable reports. He would not be disappointed!

Also on these tours were the guys who kept the show moving and dealt with the logistics – the "roadies" – and they caused constant problems for the management and for us. Some of them were real prima donnas. Even if they had only one spotlight to control they would make a real song and dance about their perceived importance and any problems they might find. These roadies needed constant stroking and were the bane of our lives on tour. I remember once that a particular band member was really irritated by the spotlight so he climbed the ladder to the gantry to speak with the roadie in charge, who was really rude to him and shirty because he was invading his space and telling him what to do with his spotlight! If it hadn't been for that singer and the band, this guy wouldn't even have had a job! Yet he was so touchy about his little domain. Most of these roadies were heavy drug users and went about surrounded by a haze of pot, like scruffy fishing vessels chugging through fog.

Not all the bands that I toured with were hard work. The Bee Gees were quite special in their attitude towards their support staff. One night, when performing on the last day of the BBC Radio One Roadshow in the south-west of England, they called us all up onto the stage to join them in the number "You win again". There was me, little Billy, up on the stage in front of thirty thousand cheering fans, singing my heart out with the rest. Following an earlier European tour, Barry Gibb, one of the band's founding members, began to battle with a serious back problem, which required surgery. In addition, he also suffered from arthritis, and at one point it was so severe that it was doubtful whether he would be able to play guitar for much longer.

The management had put the word out that we were to keep anyone from hurting Barry's back any more than it had been already. Well, in the carnival atmosphere of the finale, one of our team, an ex-Royal Marine named Michael, took this command like a red rag to a bull. He decided to have some fun with poor old Barry and during the number up on the stage he began slapping him on the back in time with the refrain "You win again". I was mad with him while trying my best to smile and perform the song, and hissed at Michael out of the corner of my mouth, "Leave his back alone, you idiot!" It was just surreal.

The Bee Gees were quite conservative by celebrity standards, and the night before the finale Michael had already shocked them rigid in a hotel bar. As we were in the southwest, which is the home of the Marines, Michael had invited some of his ex-military and serving mates to join him in the bar, where Jerry and I and the Bee Gees were relaxing after their concert. Michael and I were on a day off so we were free to drink a few. Steve Wright from BBC Radio One was there with his Roadshow team. He and his posse made their mark on the station's breakfast, afternoon, and weekend shows, and won a stack of awards, including Best DJ of the Year, as voted by readers of the *Sun* and by the *Daily Mirror* Readers' Poll, and by *Smash Hits* in 1994. His PA at the time was a guy who was quite crazy. He drank up his pint and then proceeded to eat the glass! I was downing Jack Daniel's and cokes, and the atmosphere in this five-star hotel bar was getting quite lively.

The Royal Marines have a tradition they call "naked bar", where, if one of them shouts out those words, the rest of them have to take all their clothes off and drink their pints naked. The hotel bar was quite select, really, very upmarket, and so it was a total shock to us all when one of these guys yelled "Naked bar!" Michael and the rest of them stripped off completely and stood there supping up, completely in the buff! Jerry and the Bee Gees didn't know where to put themselves, and neither did I. The band's manager got us boys to hustle them quickly out, followed by a line of "tutting" ladies like a gaggle of geese fleeing an invading fox. Michael and his mates crooned on, the strains of "Zulu warrior" rising from stark naked Marines creating a musical background for the departing guests! Needless to say, Jerry was not amused. But it was an unforgettable night.

At that stage I was riding high on this touring bandwagon. I felt untouchable after my early disillusionment. I was king of the castle now. The money we were earning was fantastic and the atmosphere inside the artificial bubble we were all living in was amazing. I did not envy the celebrities their public profile. The constant scrutiny by the media so that your life is no longer your own must be unbearable. But I did envy them their privileged place in the hedonistic lifestyle of the tours, in which they appeared to be free to do anything they wanted without worrying about the consequences. That was not true, of course, because there was a price to be paid, as the later lives of many of these celebs was to demonstrate all too clearly, but at that stage of the game I was hooked on all this excess. This proved to be my downfall, really, because, just as I had at Sandhurst, I lapsed into arrogance. I thought I could be whatever I wanted to be in this world, but I overstepped the mark one time too many.

I was supposed to turn up on a Friday afternoon in London to meet Jerry to discuss hotel security for an upcoming tour, but I made the excuse that I was ill. The reality was that I had gone on an all-day drinking session with one of the gangsters whom I was starting to get to know quite well, and stupidly I had taken my drinking pals to the Hard Rock Café in the afternoon and acted as if I owned the place. I thought nobody would see me and so I turned up there drunk. In my arrogance I started introducing these gangsters to one or two of my friends who worked there. Suddenly, to my horror and consternation, in walked Jerry. He looked me up and down and said sadly, "I hope you enjoyed your day, son, because you will not be going on tour on Monday."

That was it. I was off the tours and grounded. At that precise moment I didn't care, but once I began to sober up and the drugs began to wear off I realized that I had blown it because it wasn't just about going back on tour. I was beginning to realize what I had become and to face the fact that I wasn't a success: I was a failure. In a sense I had been sacked, although Jerry had a lot of time for me and gave me a lot of support again afterwards, but the damage had been done to our relationship. I was off the tours but Jerry kept me on the books and in work, mainly doing mundane jobs around London's recording studios, concert venues such as the Royal Albert Hall, and so on, but it wasn't the same because I knew I had let him down and he knew it too.

It was also at that point that our first son, Jordan, was born, and I began to realize that I was now failing Bev and my newborn son. My attitude was getting out of hand for my privileged role on the tours. I was hammered with drink or drugs just too often to be overlooked. He had grounded me. I was stunned and devastated, but unrepentant.

20

A CRIMINAL IN ALL BUT NAME

Once Jerry had sacked me from touring and sent me back to London, my attitude became increasingly resentful and underhand. I was selling and supplying drugs by this stage and therefore starting to mix with some very unsavoury people.

Jerry was such a warm-hearted guy, and from the kindness of his heart he gave me chance after chance to shape up and sort myself out. Plácido Domingo was scheduled to sing at the Royal Albert Hall to raise money for the José Carreras International Leukaemia Foundation, and it was to be a prestigious dinner-jacket event. Jerry had asked me to be there, so I changed out of my suit into a dinner jacket in the briefing room and left to be with the star tenor and conductor himself. Once I had left the room, amazingly Jerry put on my discarded suit jacket by mistake and found a stash of forged blank MOT certificates that I had squirrelled away in the inside pocket to sell later on.

He was furious with me. He tore me off a strip, pointing out that he had gone out on a limb to give me another chance and here I was jeopardizing the whole reputation of his company as well as breaking the law. I guess, looking back, that it was meant to be that Jerry would find out about my criminal activities. I mean, how likely was it that he would put on my discarded jacket by mistake? He grabbed the bunch of forms and asked, "Whose are these forms? And what are ye planning to do with them, eh? You know I could have yer arrested for this!" I just shrugged and made out that I didn't really know, because I felt so bad about letting him down.

Jerry Judge was a father figure to many young celebrities then, as he still is today. I didn't realize how lucky I was to have him taking an interest in my well-being. Just as Sergeant Partington had been in the forces, Jerry was the man I really wanted to please, so I really regretted what I had done, but unfortunately not enough to change my ways.

****

While I was still working for Jerry I began to come into contact with people from the underworld of drugs and crime. I had started off by just indulging in what I saw my clients doing, but pretty soon, because of the frame of mind I was in, drug use became the overriding factor in my life. I began taking quite a lot myself, mainly cocaine and ecstasy, and from there I spiralled down to smoking crack. Crack is a crystallized form of cocaine that has undergone a certain chemical process, and it is believed that the name comes from the cracking sounds it makes while being smoked. It is highly addictive and dangerous. I also started taking heroin.

Obviously I needed to find a source for all these illegal substances, and I started spending a lot of money in the process. Within the music and film industries drugs have to come from somewhere and so I was introduced to some of the key figures in the London underworld. One or two of them took me under their wing a bit, perhaps seeing in me a conduit for getting their drugs into the hands of the celebrities I was guarding. Once I was sent back to London by the security firm I also started dealing in counterfeit money on the side. My part was to collect or deliver thousands of pounds' worth of counterfeit money to various outlets in and around the city.

✳✳✳

It was a dark and depressing day, drizzling at first and threatening to rain more heavily. I was finding it very hard to drag myself out of bed these days anyway, but when the day was as black and miserable as this it was well-nigh impossible. When the phone rang I recognized the number and answered straight away, as these people could be seriously violent if you let them down. A gruff voice ordered me to go and pick up a package of forged money at a service station off the M25, and informed me that a car was already on its way to pick me up. I got up, showered pretty smartly, and waited for the toot of the horn outside.

I knew the guy who was driving as we had worked together before, so we drove in silence to the parking area off the motorway and waited nervously for the gang to appear. As paranoia and fear got hold of my imagination once again, it was easy to believe that the passing groups of motorists heading into the services were all plain-clothes detectives, on the lookout for me. Finally a smart-looking Vauxhall Vectra pulled in alongside us. I stepped gingerly out of our car and crossed over to the door of the Vectra. The mean-looking guy who was driving it motioned for me to get in so I slid into the passenger seat. The smell of tobacco smoke, beer, and stale sweat almost made me gag. The envelope containing the cash was lying at the base of the gearstick. What I saw next made me freeze with fear. Just to the right of the gearstick was a gun. My neck went cold, goose bumps stood out on my forearms, and I stuttered in an attempt to speak, but he cut me off.

"Shut up," he said, "it's all there. Don't count it here. Take it and get out!" Needing no second instruction I grabbed the envelope of cash and scurried back to our vehicle, relieved that there had been no need for him to use that gun. We took the money back with us to a really bad guy in the city to do the deal. By that stage I knew that I was mixing with some very dodgy and dangerous people. My own need for drugs, though, kept driving me deeper.

None of this came easily to me at first. I was in the thick of an emotional turmoil, facing the dilemma of my increasing disloyalty to Bev, Jordan, and everything I knew to be right and decent. My training in the army, not to mention my upbringing, meant that I still had a conscience, although I was starting to shut its voice up fairly effectively. It was a slippery slope down which I was skidding but I justified my actions to myself by reasoning that I was really living the life. I had access to cocaine and had these gangsters depending on me and even looking after me, and then there were all those celebrities that I was meeting, so I told myself, "Surely it will all turn out well." Then "the Law" started taking notice of me.

****

Scotland Yard's famous Flying Squad knew most of the criminals I was working with and would visit them now and again. Sometimes, fearing that the police would come while I was with them, the gangsters would tell me to shove the money or drugs down my trousers and leave. For a while I managed to escape from arrest in this way, but it was only a matter of time.

On one occasion I ran into the police again on a night out in the West End. I had gone to Ronnie Scott's jazz café with another friend. Through my work I had access to the club and that night I got extremely drunk. Sutton in Surrey was my home in those days, which is at the end of an underground railway line south of London. I had planned to get a taxi back there and so hailed one, and then fell into a drunken stupor, so when I woke up in the back of the taxi it wasn't at Sutton at all. It was at Morden, which is several miles away. Apparently the taxi driver had been trying to wake me up and when he failed to rouse me he had contacted the police.

Officers got into the cab and tried to wake me up by slapping my face and shaking me. Eventually I grasped what was going on and realized that I did not have the money to pay the fare. I protested to the driver that he was supposed to take me home, because I knew that I had thousands of pounds in my drawer – not all of it legal tender, of course.

Unfortunately the police accompanied me home, as they thought I might run away. One of the officers actually came with me into the house. I was living in one of the gangsters' mother's houses at that time, as Bev and Jordan had gone back to Wales. I told the officer that I would just go and get the money from my room but he insisted on coming with me. Now this presented me with a big problem because I knew that my top drawer was absolutely stuffed with wads of cash. Some of it was counterfeit and the rest was mainly the proceeds of drug deals. I was still fairly drunk, so, with the policeman standing behind me, I pulled the drawer open to reveal my stash of illegal money. Amazingly, he was looking around the room at that moment, perhaps seeking out anything illegal. He was looking for evidence of skulduggery while all the time it was right under his nose in my top drawer. On the left-hand side of the drawer was my "good" money, so I pulled out some notes and said, "Yeah, I've got it", and we went back down to the waiting taxi. I was sweating buckets by that time but got away with it.

Another day I got taken in for questioning about two stolen Suzuki Vitara jeeps that I was actually trying to sell to two Portuguese brothers in the West End. The police knew that I was involved, but in the end they had insufficient evidence to proceed. I was lucky – but was fast becoming a marked man.

By this time people in the West End of London knew me for all the wrong reasons. If I went to a bar the staff would check my money by holding it up to the light. I was even using stolen credit cards. In those days you could put a card behind the bar and then just drink away while they charged it to the card. I used stolen credit cards for that purpose and others.

Then my criminality became violent. I took on another job from a Turkish guy who sold hot cockles on the street corner outside Planet Hollywood. He had got to know me as a bit of a fly guy, along with a few of the other boys, and he knew we could get things done. He had a problem with another Turkish man who owned a photo lab in Caledonian Road in North London and he asked if we would go and sort him out, and he'd pay us cash. He wanted him beaten up and the photo lab with all its chemicals trashed so that the business would be ruined. We did both aspects of the job for cash. I was now sinking into the really seedy side of crime, and it was to become a regular way of life for me. Life was just crazy then, really mad days and nights.

At that stage I was high on drugs and alcohol but I was also training quite a lot in order to put on a bit of weight. I was very conscious of my image as a hard man so there was quite a bit of steroid use involved too. Tanning myself on the sunbeds by day and pumping weights and shooting steroids into my rump by night were routine for me then. I was "stacking", which is injecting steroids and also taking them by mouth, to build weight and boost muscle bulk. Gradually I became really massive, out of all proportion to my build.

On another job we went down to Dagenham where a boy owed a few thousand pounds to a drug dealer. A group of us went down to give him a good beating and I always remember that day because we nearly got caught by the police once again. It was in the early hours of the morning and the dustbin men were out doing their collection run on this particular street. One of our boys was carrying a baseball bat but when we got to the door there was no answer. By then the bin men had been alerted to the fact that there was a fracas going on around this house and they had contacted the police. As we got into the car and reached the end of the road the police were racing up with their blue lights flashing. Then, ironically, they got held up by the bin lorry, so we shot off in the opposite direction. You can imagine the frustration in the police car as we sped away, sheltered by a ponderous truck! After a few miles we pulled into a pub car park and went in for a few beers to relax. This was the crazy world I had become part of by that stage, and for some bizarre reason I thought I was untouchable, a real king of the castle.

Throughout all this time Bev was back in a house in Sidcup but I have to admit that by now she was spending a lot of time in Wales, and it was during this period that she went back there permanently. In a sense she gave up on me and took the boys (we had by this time had a second son, Jack) back to her parents. I was losing such a lot without even realizing it.

It was only by the mercy of God that I didn't get a prison sentence at that stage because I could have gone down for the things I was doing. Savage assaults, handling forged money, and drug dealing were all serious offences that carried long prison sentences. It wasn't because I was careful that I didn't get caught. I was so careless, in fact, that some of the heavies I worked for used to warn me that my attitude would get me into trouble.

"Stop being the wide guy," they told me. The guys who made it to the top in this world were the ones who stayed below the radar. I was too much of a good-time Charlie for their liking and was drawing unwanted attention to them. "Now wind yer neck in!" they warned me.

When I was on the cocaine and the steroids, with all these heavy guys around me, I thought I was above anybody's reach. I was to find out how wrong I was the hard way.

21

SCOTLAND AND ATTEMPTED SUICIDE

Once Bev had gone and I had lost the job with Jerry, all my anchors were cut and I really started to drift. I made my way back to Wales and then moved to Scotland and briefly found work, ironically enough, with the Prison Service. After that fell through, as things usually did for me then, I started to do some work with a criminal gang in Peterhead.

This led to another brush with the law. I was arrested on suspicion of the importation and supply of drugs. I had just come back from a Scotland vs Wales rugby match at Murrayfield Stadium in Edinburgh, which I had attended with my dad. That was the day I told him that Bev and I had split up. It was a dreadful day, on which I had just poured out the situation and then seen him off and got back on the train heading to where I was staying in Peterhead.

As I arrived home a neighbour said, "Oh, people in suits have been round to see you. I think they were police or something," and my heart sank. I phoned the police station to find out what they wanted and before I had even put the phone down the cop cars were there, swarming around the house like angry bees round a hive. Two CID officers in suits burst in and, taking hold of my arm, said, "Billy Gilvear, you're under arrest on suspicion of conspiracy to import drugs", and then they read me my rights. They searched the house and asked if I had got anything illegal in there and I said, "No", but then I remembered I had steroids galore. Despite the fact that they were for my personal use the police still took them away. I always remember that they checked my pockets, which contained a meat and potato pie left over from the rugby match. I chuckled at that because the CID man got the mixture all over his hand.

Then they handcuffed me and pushed me into the back seat of one of their cars to take me down for extensive questioning. They did not charge me then, but warned me to keep away from a certain man whom they were watching, and for whom I had been doing some jobs. As they did so I realized for the first time how big this guy was on the Scottish crime scene.

Despite this scare, I carried on working with various gangsters up there at the time, who were planning a massive importation of cannabis from Holland using one of the many fishing boats in that area. Peterhead and Aberdeen were chosen because they were the main fishing ports. It was a huge job, as there was a high tonnage of cannabis expected, worth millions of pounds. I got caught up in it, though not as a prominent player, about halfway through the operation. It was a big co-operative venture between Dutch and Scottish gangs. Some of the guys involved were among Britain's strongest men at the time, often seen on television taking part in competitions of physical strength but leading a double life. The skipper of the fishing vessel turned Queen's Evidence halfway through the operation and began working for Customs and Excise. As a result the whole team were arrested and remanded in custody at Shotts Prison, which is situated in countryside south of the M8 motorway near the Lanarkshire village of the same name.

****

A fellow called Andy rang me because I was working with the gangs up there as a doorman, collecting money. He let me know that the skipper's wife had quite a reputation for sleeping with other men while her husband was away at sea. He wanted me to get involved in the operation by seducing her, taking a kind of hidden recording device with me, in order to get out of her the fact that her husband had turned Queen's Evidence right from the start and had actually been acting as an agent provocateur. If I could get this information from her then the gangs' lawyers would argue in court that the authorities had acted illegally, hoping to get the gang members off "scot" free.

I did what I was told, and got the information they wanted, but it did them no good in the end. Some gang members got out but half the team were sentenced heavily. That night, however, became a stitch-up for me because Andy thought he could also make money for himself from the skipper while I was sleeping with his wife, by letting him know what I was up to, but not why. I thought I was safe in his house (because there was a 2-mile [3.2 km] exclusion zone around it into which the skipper was not allowed to pass), but when Andy told him I was sleeping with his wife he jumped out of police protective custody and headed for home.

I was in the room half naked while she was in bed when the skipper turned up at the door. I was terrified and expected him to have a gun and shoot me, but after a short exchange of blows

I managed to make good my escape. I realized afterwards that Andy had done that just so that he could extract a few pounds from the skipper. In this world that I had joined you could not trust anybody, even those who claimed that they were on your side. It was a filthy business, and one that I am truly ashamed of now, but at the time I was completely immersed in it. I saw that there was no honour at all among thieves and that they would betray me at any stage for their own ends. It was dog eat dog and, although I was not a Christian, I knew it was all so wrong.

✳✳✳✳

The people that I was collecting money from were mostly drug dealers themselves and therefore potentially violent people just like me. They were selling the drugs but keeping the money, and they had no intention of giving it back to my boss, so collecting from them was like going to war. In those days I used to sleep with a baseball bat under my bed because at any time the guys could turn on me.

It was gang warfare just as you see on television. Sometimes we had to go in heavily, smashing doors down and screaming like banshees, terrifying anybody inside, women and children included. If the target was not in we would smash some possessions up and tell them, "We'll be back, so make sure the money's there!"

Once we were sent to collect in Fraserburgh, another town in the north-east of Scotland. The person who owed our boss the money lived on a stereotypical sort of Scottish council estate: drab, uniform, and defaced with graffiti, abandoned cars, and discarded rubbish. As we sat in the car watching his property from nearby we saw the target and a friend disappear round the back of his house. We suspected that these guys would be "tasty" – in other words they would do whatever they had to do to defend their territory, including using weapons. I turned to my friend Gordon and said, "This is big. Now we have to go in heavy." Gordon had a baseball bat ready and I had taken a diving knife with me, not dissimilar to the bayonets we had used in the army, but with a bigger grip. We followed them round the back to find that one of them was already inside the back door while the second stood nearby. Immediately Gordon whacked the one outside the door with the bat, breaking his arm and smashing him to the ground. Meanwhile, the main target was reaching inside the house to grab something from the shelf just inside the door. I didn't know if it was cutlery, a knife, or even a gun. I lunged at him and stuck my knife right into the side of his outstretched arm. I just stabbed him and then drew the knife out again and pulled the guy back away from the shelf. He fell heavily to the floor with blood spurting from his arm. Recounting these things disgusts me now, but I remember also smashing him in the head with my boot while he was down and wounded. All we were interested in was overpowering these two men and getting our money. So by then we had a guy on the ground outside with a broken arm and we had one stabbed inside the house, both of them screaming in pain. Neither of them had the money but they knew where they could get some, so we took the one with the broken arm in the car and drove away. We left the bleeding stab victim to sort himself out while we forced his mate to a cash machine, where he got our cash.

As we drove away from this crime scene we shouted with relief, but I knew that I had crossed a line again. Inside all of us there is a voice of conscience that tells us when we breach boundaries such as this. In my later work as a prison chaplain I would hear many similar stories of men and women who sank to the depths that I did and just knew in their heart of hearts that they were wrong. But at that stage, like many of them, I silenced that nagging voice and carried on. Yet we had done the job because, if we hadn't, we ourselves would have been badly beaten by our own employers. We were in a "Catch 22" situation and had little choice. I knew that it was a question of the survival of the fittest and that if I didn't smash these people then I was going down, and I didn't want that to happen. At that time in the 1990s guns were starting to be much more common and, although I never used a gun on anyone, I was around people who did, and there was always the possibility that we would face them in our line of work. We didn't go in with the intention of killing anyone, but we did plan to disable them temporarily so that they couldn't use a weapon against us. It was that kind of mentality: self-protection and using violence to pre-empt further violence. None of that excuses any of what we did, but it may help to explain our twisted thinking.

✳✳✳✳

I was in a very dark place. Owing to a fight in a pub my nose and mouth had been badly smashed by the very people I thought were my mates. My world seemed totally corrupt and lonely.

Ironically, one of my sisters was working for the police in Scotland at that time. One weekend I had nothing planned so she invited me to meet her in Callander for a couple of days to go white-water rafting with the police team! Throughout the entire drug importation job in which I had become involved, the Scottish crime squad were active – the top guys in the Scottish crime-busting fraternity – and my sister knew who I was involved with. She contacted me and told me that the guy I was working with was really bad news and extremely dangerous. She warned me that if I didn't change my ways I was going to be either badly hurt by them or arrested again by the police.

She took me to the raft races just so that I could get active on the river and get some exercise. Once I got there, though, I could not believe that I was rafting for the police team! It was all a bit unreal. I thought, "What am I doing here with my nose broken, messing around with these police people?" I had a few beers afterwards but it was at this point that the wheels started to come off in my mind. I thought, "I've lost everything – Bev, my sons, my dignity, and now the gang guys have turned on me so that I have literally nowhere to go." I didn't want to move back home to stay with my parents so I decided that I couldn't go on any more. At that point I just wanted to crawl away and die.

After the raft race we headed for my parents' home, where Mum gave us lunch. My sister was there with another policeman, who eventually became her husband. I just kept up the jokey exterior that was my best defence in circumstances like this. Afterwards the three of us went out for some drinks, which was never a good idea where I was concerned. I got home really loaded up with spirits and went to a room upstairs in the house where I could take an overdose. I took a massive dose of pain-killing medication and other drugs, and topped it off with more whisky.

I remember nothing after that until I came out of a coma in the Intensive Care Unit at the Stirling Royal Infirmary.

Apparently I was there for a day or two before starting to come round, and gradually I began to focus on my mum, who was at my bedside. Mum had realized what I had done at once, because she said that I had come down to the dining room and started apologizing to her and my sister for even breathing. Seeing my distress and noticing my dreadful appearance, they kept talking to me while waiting for an ambulance to come, and got me admitted to hospital. My dad was away in the Highlands at that time doing some work for the mission that employed him.

As I began to rise from the depths of unconsciousness I became aware of my mum stroking the back of my hand and speaking to me. Well, she wasn't talking to me, really, but to God and the devil! She was telling the devil that he couldn't have me because she had given me to God before I was born. Then she reminded God of the promise she felt he had given her that one day I would be a preacher!

As I began to surface, she told me, "Billy, I've got to tell you this. God still loves you and he's told me that one day you're going to preach the gospel. I know you don't want to hear this but…" then she choked up, and when she could she just repeated her total love for me and her confidence that I would recover. I wished that I could believe her, but I was just gutted to still be alive. I had failed again, but not as badly as I was about to.

22

WALES AGAIN

Once I had completed detox in a psychiatric hospital I moved in with my parents for a while, but was soon feeling pretty fed up living back at home and decided to go back down to Wales and find Bev again. It was coming up to her birthday, so I rang her and she agreed to meet me at the station.

She was just sitting there in the car as if I was coming home from work at the end of a normal day, and I hopped into the passenger seat. I noted the arousing aroma of her perfume in the car and it immediately evoked sadness in me at what I had lost. As she looked back over her right shoulder to pull out into the traffic she asked how I was, so I started to tell her a little bit of what had just been happening and all that I had been through.

As I was speaking her face crumpled and tears began to flow. Bev wiped her face with her arm so that she could see through the windscreen and keep driving. Along with her sadness and distress she became angry because my mum and dad had not told her the full extent of what was going on. They had wanted to protect her and Jordan and Jack from yet another dark episode in my troubled life, but Bev felt that although we were separated I was still "Dad" to her children. She also still felt a bit responsible towards me. She explained that she still had some love for me but not as her husband. Her feelings then were more a mixture of pity and regret. I was not honest with her and so she was not aware at that stage that I had got so deeply involved with drug dealing, drug taking, violence, and gang culture. Mainly out of pity, I expect, we had a brief go at being together again in Wales, for the sake of the boys, but in our naïvety we didn't realize that even bigger trouble lay ahead.

Bev must have wondered what on earth she was letting herself in for by taking me back into her home in Cwmbran, but I tried to adapt to a normal life again. I did my best to keep my nose clean and be a good dad to Jordan and Jack. I still wasn't well and visited a psychiatrist once a week. Bev would drive me there to make sure I kept my appointments and see that I took my medication, but it wasn't easy for her. It was not enough either, because by this stage I was overwhelmed with guilt, regret, and remorse. I never felt good enough for her kindness, which had been the story right the way through my life. This was because of the early days at home and all the violence and toughness since.

Unfortunately, and unbeknown to her, Bev was living right next door to a woman whose husband was a major drug dealer. She was a lovely lady and a good friend, but her bloke was really messed up. I spent lots of time hanging around the house and so it was not long before he and I got chatting. It turned out that he was a major importer of drugs and was dealing them as well. In a strange irony I would later discover that he had served five years in the Guernsey Prison for importing drugs to the island where I would one day become the prison chaplain, but all that lay far in the future. When Bev and his wife were out, he would say to me, "Here is a little something to help you on your way", and slip me a package of drugs, which I foolishly took, mixing them with my own prescribed antipsychotics – an explosive combination.

Slowly and with sinister predictability I got back into the whole drugs and drinking scene. Once more I became selfish and devious towards Bev and the boys. Even though I'd been given yet another chance at family life the drugs had regained their hold on me and finally Bev had no alternative other than to push me out of the door and divorce me.

There was no going back. I realized too late that the neighbour I had thought was helping me was actually an instrument of my destruction and an enemy of my life and family.

Sullen and bitter, I rented a room in a house in Bassaleg, a small suburb on the west side of the city of Newport, in South Wales. I got a job in a restaurant but unfortunately it was quite a high-class restaurant with an à la carte menu and society dinners. It was hard work, and I was drinking to excess and doing a lot of drugs, so it wasn't long before the wheels really came off. On one occasion we were holding a bit of a staff party at one of their houses nearby and a colleague really wound me up when I asked him for a light for my cigarette. I remember trying to get to him in the kitchen, with others holding me back.

Furious, I shrugged them off and pulled the kitchen door off its hinges and he was enraged by this and just lost it with me, lunging at my face, so I grabbed him and threw him to the ground. Then I sat on top of him and started to pummel his head with my fists as all my frustration and anger boiled over and poured into this poor man's body. I just couldn't stop, and kept smashing his head even when he put his hands up to cover his face. It took three of the bigger guys there to pull me off him. In the end I crashed my way out of the house, still seething, but aware that I could easily have killed that man. As it was, his injuries turned out to be bad enough. He had a fractured cheekbone and his eye socket was pushed right in, not to mention a broken jaw and nose. He also lost a couple of teeth and his face was completely deformed, though I didn't find that out until later.

The next day I learned that I had been sacked from my job and banned from every pub in Bassaleg. I had become known in the area as a thug and a hooligan. As I could no longer drink in the town I started taking taxis into Newport. One night I took exception to what a taxi driver said about one of my mates and, while he was actually driving, I punched him twice, yanking on the handbrake. I had no intention of robbing him but he had really annoyed me and I wanted revenge. I smacked him in the face and when I pulled up the handbrake the car spun in the road and stopped. The other two guys in the back seat got out and ran but I was just holding this guy's head and hitting it on the dashboard, shouting, "I'm going to kill you!" At this point my anger was once again totally out of control.

When I heard about the injuries my colleague had suffered I expected to be arrested, and waited every day for the police to arrive. Finally, about a week after the assault, the police arrested me. They came to the house, cautioned me, and took me down to the police station. It was a Saturday morning and they locked me in the cells to cool off. I was a heavy smoker then so I was allowed to go out into the yard with a couple of other prisoners to have a cigarette, and I just sat there with an angry sneer on my lips. I was full of all the nervous bravado of the foolish newly arrested man. The police got me a lawyer and he came to meet me, but he did not hold out much hope for me. Telling me the extent of the victim's injuries, he explained that I would probably be charged with causing grievous bodily harm (GBH), which is very serious. He thought I would be facing a custodial sentence and told me to be very careful what I admitted to. When the officers came to accompany me to the interview room I was still feeling fairly arrogant, though a little shaken by the attitude of my brief. I sat before the CID officers, who questioned me for hours. They had photographs from the hospital of the poor complainant's injuries.

The sergeant in charge looked a mean piece of work himself and had probably been in a few fights too. He was a chubby man in his early fifties but his bulk was not all fat. His gnarled face and slightly bent nose seemed to match his cynical attitude and tough-guy approach. He growled at me and said, "We put it to you, Mr Gilvear, that this was not just four punches to the head, as you say, but many more."

My defence was that I was a boxer and so there was a possibility that there might have been more, but also that the other guy had instigated the whole thing and I was acting in self-defence! I claimed that these were mitigating circumstances, and at my pre-trial hearing I was asked if I wanted the case to go to crown court or to be dealt with in the magistrates' court. I didn't know what to say so I turned to my lawyer. He whispered emphatically in my ear, "Look, I've no chance of getting you off in a crown court. If you face a jury you might get a long sentence for this, but at magistrates' court I've got half a chance because there's no jury and we can kind of work the magistrate, you know", adding a conspiratorial wink. He thought that if a jury were to see the pictures of the victim's wounds they would convict me out sympathy for him and I would have no chance.

I opted for the magistrates' court and so the trial date was set. I was trying to tell myself that I didn't fear jail, but my head had completely gone, especially once I started drying out without my much-needed drink and drugs. By this time I was way beyond any human means of help, but I know now that both Mum and Dad were praying for me and so was Bev, who had started to believe the Christian message herself. Mum told me much later that she felt that there was a kind of inevitability that my lifestyle would lead to this, and she was at peace in her heart that God was at work. She felt that perhaps this was what it would take to yank me out of the insane world I was living in. Not me. I was getting very agitated and trying desperately to psych myself up for what lay ahead. I didn't relish losing my freedom.

On the day of the trial my friend Dave was with me. He had come up the night before to stay with me. I didn't have much in the world beyond a few basic belongings, but I'd packed my case with what few clothes I had and given it to him. If I was sentenced to jail he was to take my case over to Bev's.

Dave stayed with me as I went to face the first day of the trial. When we arrived at the court building there was a white prison van parked outside, with its sinister little windows covered by bars. I was having a last cigarette and I said to Dave, "I'll be in that later, won't I?"

Kindly he replied, "Oh, you don't know, mate, anything can happen," but we both knew the score. The case before mine had run over so we were only called in for a little bit of the trial and had to come back the next day. When we did, still full of apprehension, we sensed that the atmosphere in the court had changed. Something strange had happened, because the witnesses who were due to testify for the prosecution all decided they didn't want to give evidence. Now I can say categorically before God that I put no pressure on anybody. I didn't have any friends who could do so on my behalf, either, so this was a really mysterious – though welcome – turn of events for me and my defence lawyer. One of them announced that she was going off to university and didn't want to get embroiled in a court case at all. Another just did not want to be involved, and said that we should sort it out between us.

I was very arrogant in front of the magistrates and I remember my lawyer saying when I sat down, "Hey, Billy. You need to wind your neck in because you're not doing yourself any favours with this attitude. With all the evidence they have and the way you're behaving, you're just going to go down in that white van, so please stop this now!" He seemed to think that we might have half a chance because the prosecution's witnesses were dropping out, so I tried to shape up.

The trial went on that day with the lawyers questioning me and then him. Then, as it was Friday, the court was adjourned and they said we would reconvene on the Monday, which then got delayed to the Tuesday because of another case. In the meantime the plaintiff's lawyer phoned my lawyer to see if they could do a deal out of court. They had realized that with the witnesses out of the way there was a chance that the complainant would not get what he wanted out of the case, and that I might get away with it. They wanted me to admit my guilt and agree to be bound over for a year by the court, but my lawyer would not countenance this. Even though their case was seriously weakened, he reasoned that I would still get a criminal record, and he wanted to go for a complete "not guilty" verdict. I was amazed, because I knew I *was* guilty, but I was just so glad that this was the way things were moving.

In the end the prosecution lawyer went back to confer with his client and then notified my brief that they agreed. My lawyer phoned me and said, "Billy, the case has been dismissed. You're a free man!" I couldn't believe it. I had resigned myself to being carted off to prison, probably to do a minimum of eight months because it was the magistrates' court. If I had been found guilty in the crown court I'd have probably got two to three years. And I was a free man!

Yet I was more miserable at that time than I had ever been in my life. I felt abandoned by Bev and my parents, bereft of even my best friend, Dave, who had returned home after the trial, and thus totally alone in the world. What I didn't know was that, just around the corner, the most amazing experience of my life was about to begin. In a stable.

23

FARMYARD MIRACLE

What little money I did get in those days was spent on beer and drugs, so there was hardly anything left for food. I became emaciated and desperately depressed as well as paranoid and aggressive. It would be only a matter of time before I got into another scrap and all hope of leniency or freedom would be gone. My body was so broken-down that my skin would erupt in boils, abscesses, and rashes, and I scratched myself incessantly. I used to drown my sorrows at what we called "the TA" – not the Territorial Army but the Tredegar Arms – which was the only pub in Bassaleg from which I was not completely barred. The landlord was wary of me, however, and I knew that I had to behave or he would be calling in back-up from the local police.

By early afternoon, as usual, I was hanging out at the bar close on the heels of the lunchtime trade. I had nowhere else to go and nothing to do but feel sorry for myself. Then a guy called Chris, whom I knew and who lived nearby, came over and drank with me. He told me about a relative of his, Gwyn, who with his brother, Robert, ran a farm not far away and needed help. "Why don't you go up there and see him, Billy? I have heard that they might have some accommodation at the farm too." I was immediately interested because the room I was dossing in was awful, and I thought, "Well at least it can't be any worse than this." So I went off up the hill just outside the town to the huge homestead that is Croesheolydd Farm, and there I met the people in whose company my whole future direction would be changed.

Gwyn and Robert were fine. They were among the three sons and two daughters brought up by Nancy Williams and her late husband on the farm. They just seemed like decent working blokes with a flair for running the dairy farm following the death of their father, and doing all sorts of other work like landscape gardening and small-time building and repairs.

The main farmhouse was built in 1620 and has been extended many times so that it looks a bit of a hotchpotch of buildings now, some parts plastered white and others made out of typical Welsh stone. It sits neatly among the rolling hills just above Bassaleg, and nowadays it also offers a man-made lake and a tourist caravan park.

During the two and a half years that I was to spend there I got to know it very well, and I worked hard in that place. I planted many of the trees among which the caravanners spend their holidays today. Back then it was just a working farm surrounded by fields and woods. Outhouses, barns, and stables enclosed a large sloping farmyard at the base of which stood a huge slurry tank beside its collecting pit, which was to feature centre stage in my plans for self-destruction.

The main house still has many original features, such as a wide, elegant staircase and huge baronial fireplaces. Some of these are overlooked by brooding stag-head trophies and girded with slate hearths. The low doorways and beams everywhere on the ground floor make it look its age, but the many rooms upstairs are large and homely, with fairly up-to-date fittings. Outside the back door, standing alone away from the house, was an outside toilet reserved for the workmen, which we nicknamed "the Tardis", after Dr Who's time machine. The first time I went to see the farm I used it before I entered the kitchen, and as I stepped through the back door of the house I thought that I had landed on a distant but vaguely familiar planet. It immediately intimidated me.

I walked into the kitchen to meet Rob and Gwyn's mum, Nancy. She was pleasant enough but I was confronted straight away by posters proclaiming slogans like "Smile, God loves you" and "Jesus is Lord!" To my horror I felt that I had been plunged back into a scene from my childhood, and I was genuinely worried. I nearly ran outside to re-enter the Tardis and try again! The guys just laughed and told me, "Oh, don't worry about her. Mum's just a bit of a Christian fruit and nutcase, you see, and she likes to use the house for her friends from church to come and visit, but she's harmless."

I was very wary, but I have to admit that this dear old lady, who came up only to my armpit in stature and whose warm heart was as big as her grin, welcomed me into her home as if I were a long-lost son. She generously gave me a whole suite of rooms on one side of the main house, where I was in clover with my own kitchen, bedroom, and plenty of living space. Occasionally whole groups of people from nearby churches came to the farm to stay for a few days, mainly at weekends, and at times like that I tried to keep out of the way. Sometimes groups taking part in Alpha courses, designed to introduce people to the Christian faith, would come to stay at the farm for what they called "the Holy Spirit weekend".

It all seemed crazy to me. They would be singing and praying in the main rooms downstairs and, no matter how much I tried to keep my head down as I nipped through there in order to reach the main staircase, they would greet me or even pray for me out loud! I suspected that Nancy had told them she had this particularly bad lad staying there, and so they made me the target of their faith and prayers.

Despite receiving all this kindness and care, I was really miserable in that place. My behaviour was not good either and I became a cause of real concern to Nancy, who spoke to her boys about me. If she had known what I was really getting up to in my rooms she would have had even more reason to speak out, but I tried to hide the worst of it from her. Yet still she loved me and fed me on the finest food you can imagine. We were dining on the real fat of the land, with home-produced milk, butter, and cheese as well as hams, hotpots, and stews, homemade cakes, chutneys, and puddings. Nancy was an amazing cook and she seemed determined to build up my scrawny frame if nothing else.

Nancy then moved me out of the wing up into a loft bedroom where I would be a bit more contained. Up there in the loft, though, I felt like rubbish, shoved up in the attic because it was worthless. The room smelt of old things, spare things, blankets that have been stored for ages and never used, and the musty aroma of 350-year-old wooden beams and bare slates. I ran my hands over those beams sometimes, even getting splinters in my hands, and tried to draw some comfort from their antiquity and strength, but to no avail. I was constantly aware that I was a huge disappointment to everyone who cared for me, not least to my parents and my ex-wife, Bev, and my two sons. I had been stealing money from Bev even after she had taken me back into her home, and using it for drugs. I had been going missing for days on end in drug- and alcohol-induced binges until I crept back out of the gutter. I was just a real scumbag and I hated myself. I used to gaze out of the only window at the end of my loft bedroom and sob as I watched the animals in the yard below and thought how much simpler their lives were than mine. They didn't seem to worry about anything beyond their food and drink, and had none of the awful burden of guilt and regret that I was bearing.

My parents were still trying to reach me with various kinds of help, but without success. They contacted the pastor of a local Baptist church, Harry Place, and asked him to visit me at the farm. Harry rang several times but couldn't reach me because I was avoiding his calls. He made four different appointments to see me and I missed all of them! I just did not need some preacher telling me I was a mess. I knew that I was, and I wanted to end it all. I just wanted to die.

My decision to commit suicide was neither rushed nor any kind of cry for help. I thought about it deeply and with increasing determination over several weeks. I did my research on the computer down at the village library and I found out what was needed this time to make sure that I did not wake up in some psychiatric hospital as before. Hanging seemed the most likely method to be effective quickly, and the slurry tank on the farm a good prospect for privacy. Almost certainly I would not be found until it was too late. I made the noose myself out of a sturdy piece of rope and crafted it just as they had shown me on the Internet, hiding it in one of the outbuildings until it would be needed.

On the morning everything changed I discovered that I was in trouble with Nancy again. I had crept into the house in the early hours trying not to wake her, but the ancient floorboards in this centuries-old homestead were hopeless for silent creeping. In any case I was pretty spaced out, bumping into furniture and then apologizing to it noisily as I passed.

When I surfaced later in the morning I could hear her in the kitchen, and I went down to make myself a cup of coffee. The acrid smell of brass polish hit me as I entered the room. Nancy was busy shining up the brasses that she had gathered from around the house, which she did from time to time as there were plenty of them. She grimaced as I entered and went over to the sink by the kitchen window. I could feel her eyes boring into the back of my neck as I gazed innocently out through the window at the sheep grazing beyond.

"Well, Billy, you have certainly blotted your copybook again," she intoned with obvious displeasure.

"Yeah, I know; I'm sorry," was all I could manage as I turned and slipped onto one of the benches alongside the enormous table which was the centrepiece of her amazing kitchen.

In her hands she held an enormous brass kettle, the kind that would once have been hung on a spit over an open fire. It had become badly tarnished, so you could not see the original colour, but as she polished the underlying brass began to blaze as it came up sparkling clean. The stench of Brasso™ seemed to clear my head somehow, like using an inhaler after a heavy cold. Suddenly a voice spoke as clear as day in my awakening brain:

"Billy Gilvear, this kettle is your life!"

It wasn't Nancy speaking, though it seemed to me like an audible voice, and the words were then repeated: "Billy Gilvear, this kettle is your life!"

Somehow I just knew that this was God speaking to me, even though I had not heard from him for ages, if ever. I watched part of the kettle appear bright and gleaming under Nancy's hand and in a moment of understanding it just clicked for me, and I knew what God was trying to tell me. My life had become a tarnished mess and I needed a power greater than myself to clean it up, just as Nancy was renovating that kettle. I also realized for the first time that if God was on my case then there was hope.

All of a sudden the verses I had learned as a child came flooding back into my mind. I hadn't thought about them for years, but I remembered how my father used to offer me pocket money if I would memorize and repeat Bible texts. So, very unwillingly, I had given myself to parroting these passages from the Scriptures without really understanding their true meaning.

Now it was all coming back to me. "Jesus said, 'I am the way and the truth and the life: no-one comes to the Father except through me'" and "I have come that they may have life, and have it to the full." Then I recalled the words of John 3:16, which had been my father's favourite verse: "For God so loved the world that he gave his one and only Son, that whoever believes in him shall not perish but have eternal life." I also began to visualize my mother at work in the children's clubs and meetings that I had attended in my earliest days. She would get out a flannel background and put a black heart on it. Then she used to stick a red velvet cross right over it. She told the boys and girls that we all have hearts that are black with sin. I certainly knew, many years later, that mine was one of those. The red cross, she explained to their attentive little ears, represented Jesus dying at Calvary to take away all our sins.

Then Mum used to whip out a white cross and lay it over the black one to let the children know that their hearts could be clean because of what Jesus had achieved through his death, and that they could begin again.

My mind was full of all this now, and after all these years it was as if she had been talking only to me. I realized that my heart was as filthy and tarnished as that old kettle but that Christ could make me clean. After decades of darkness and confusion it was as if a veil were being lifted from my sight and I could see things clearly that I had never understood before.

I left the house that morning in a state of panic, but also elation. Panic because I did not want to miss whatever it was God might be trying to say to me, and elation because hope had been born at last in my poor despairing soul.

I headed over to a new building site that Rob was working on in Bridgend, where we were going to lay some turf, but my mind was miles away from the job. I stood in the back garden and looked up into the sky. It was a freezing cold day but bright with strong sunshine. Around me were the typical noises of a building site: a cement mixer chugged away in the background accompanied by the cymbal-like scraping of the occasional shovel. Rob was straining and groaning some way behind me as he laid out turf and packed it down, thumping it with his boots. Meanwhile I gazed into this crystal-clear sky and said, "God, if that was you this morning, you've got to help me. I'm sorry for the things that I've done… But, God, I've got nothing left!"

I was really desperate. I will never forget that moment.

All of a sudden, as I stood there staring up into the sky, all the drugs and drink in my system began to leave my body. I just felt them draining away out of me, from the head down!

It was an emotional as well as a physical sensation. All my anxiety and mental anguish just seemed to melt away and a tremendous sense of well-being poured into me. I remember feeling a deep peace that I had never known before. No drug on earth could have given me what I received in that Bridgend back garden. Then I felt as if someone gave me a hug, saying to me, "It's going to be alright, Billy". When I felt that, I was overcome with an amazing joy! I stood on that building site and experienced more happiness than I had known in my entire life, which was something I had never found on drugs. I thought to myself, "Wow! What was that?" as my whole being was overwhelmed with love and joy. The empty void inside me was beginning to be filled up with something good, like a decanter being filled with really good wine.

Despite the cold I felt that I was standing in a warm sunbeam. A great big smile crept over my face. I was starting to feel alive again. I noticed how blue the sky was looking that day, and despite the work going on around me the whole place appeared beautiful to me, like a country park! I could smell wet earth and freshly laid grass and I could have been in heaven! I turned round and Rob said to me, "What's that on your face? I've never seen you smile like that before!"

Quietly I prayed, "Thank you, Lord. Not only can I feel you but these people can see you too. Now I know that you are alive!"

I returned to the farm on cloud nine. I knew that I was changed. The old had gone and the new had come. God had spoken to me and made his love real to me, and I was utterly convinced that my life would never be the same again. As soon as I got in I told Nancy what had happened, but she was not at all surprised. She had prayed so much for God to speak to me and reveal his love to me, plus she had noticed that something strange had occurred that morning while I was watching her clean the kettle. She later told me that she could see the difference as soon as I walked through the door, and that I was not the same afterwards. I was truly transformed.

I got hold of my mobile phone and went off to find a signal so that I could let my parents know what was happening. I spoke to Dad first. "I've got something to tell you. Today I gave my heart to Jesus."

There was silence on the phone at first and then an amazing celebration. They had waited thirty years for this. My mum was hysterical and crying and we were all rejoicing together. The son that was lost had been found. The boy who was as good as dead was alive again! They were over the moon and soon made plans to come to see me to find out more. It turned out too that, even after so many rebuffs, Harry Place, the local Baptist pastor, had not been deterred and was scheduled to come to the farm again to meet me, so this time I welcomed him and spent time chatting about what had just happened to me. I was finished with the drugs and the drinking and within a couple of weeks I had even stopped smoking. Nobody told me to do that, but I felt so elated by what was going on in my life that it didn't seem right to go on abusing my poor body with this bad habit. In any case, I was starting to read the Bible and felt that God was showing me stuff and part of it was that my body had become a temple for the Holy Spirit and so I ought to start taking a bit more care of it and not fill it with noxious fumes. That made sense to me, and I wanted to co-operate with whatever God was showing me.

From this point on my room at the farm became a haven of joy to me instead of a place of abject misery. Nancy has since told me that, over the years, five of the young men who stayed in her home and worked on the farm, myself included, have become committed Christians and have gone on with God. She believes that the house is a place of healing, and so it has turned out to be, though not in any formal way. The farm also provides a base from which a great deal of support has gone out to Jewish people and in which a lot of praying has been done on behalf of Israel. It was a real "promised land" kind of place, certainly for me.

The Christian groups that used to stay there for church retreats and Alpha weekends became a source of really helpful encouragement and fellowship for me instead of a nuisance to be avoided at all costs. Through them I had access to many senior Christian leaders and pastors who had come with them to stay at the farm, and I spent many an evening chatting with them by the big fires. I felt that God was with me at the farm and even in my attic room, which from being a miserable place was transformed into a very special space. Now I would gaze out of that same end window in wonder at the creation of God. Instead of envying the animals I felt a genuine care for them and marvelled at what God had provided for the meeting of our needs. For ages afterwards I sensed his presence with me in a way that I still recall with deep gratitude. I felt that he walked with me and talked with me. It was as if he even lay down on the grass beside me when I was resting and praying outside in the better weather, and he revealed his love and his ways through the Bible as I began reading again the very book I had rejected at sixteen when I left home to join up.

24

MY NEW FAMILY

My encounter with God happened on Wednesday 6 December 2000, and immediately I sensed deep down that I would need to start going to church. It just felt like the most natural thing to do.

This was rather strange, because during my upbringing I had certainly had my fill of enforced church attendance, so it was unlikely in human terms that I would have wanted to submit myself to all that again. One thing it had taught me, though, was that being at church services was not enough to make anyone love God. I had been there in my young body but my heart and mind had been miles away. So all these years later I understood that just being in church would not change me inside or make me a child of God, because that had already happened to me at the farm. Now, since I had met with God in that backyard in South Wales, it felt so different. I was actually hungry to be with other people who knew and loved the Lord. How amazing was that? After hating being in church throughout my childhood there was now a real longing in my heart to share my faith experience with others of like mind. I wanted to tell them what had happened to me, and to listen to their stories too.

I surprised myself by the fact that I also wanted to worship God. I felt his amazing mercy towards me. He had fully accepted me back despite all my boozing and brawling and the pain I had caused others. I had come home to my real eternal Father and discovered that he had been waiting for me all the time. In my bruised and battered heart there was a song that needed to be sung, and I needed to find a safe place where I could sing it.

As the weekend approached I still did not know where I would go to worship on Sunday. I had enjoyed my chat with Harry and wondered whether the church that he looked after would be the one. On Saturday evening I crept downstairs at the farm to find Nancy and ask her which church she would recommend for me. She felt that Lliswerry Baptist Church in nearby Newport, Harry's church, would be alright. Not having been to church for so many years, I presumed that I would have to dress fairly smartly to attend.

Whenever I went as a small boy I had to wear a suit and tie. So, early on Sunday morning, I dressed in my smartest pair of dark trousers and a borrowed white shirt. I wrestled with my thin tie in front of the mirror and then went down to the kitchen to present myself to Nancy, like some kid going to a new school. I must have appeared a bit like the Ned Flanders character in *The Simpsons*[8] to her, with my hair plastered down with grease and my ill-fitting white shirt pinched at the collar by this unfamiliar fashion item. She looked at me with her warm smile and chuckled, "You know, Billy, I think you may

---

8   An American animated TV sitcom created by Matt Groening for the Fox Broadcasting Company, shown from 1989.

find that this is not what they do any more and that things are a bit different now in church." Anyway, I wanted to be sure, so off I went just as I was.

My knees were actually shaking in the car on the way there and I was as nervous as a kitten when we arrived. "Surely everybody will be staring at me," I thought, "and they'll know I am all new to this", but they weren't and they didn't. We entered what was quite a lively place of worship but one which at that point was still very much a typical South Wales Baptist church, where you sat down to sing choruses and stood up for lots of hymns, which had their numbers listed on a board on the wall behind the pulpit. There were maybe ninety to a hundred people in the congregation, of all ages, though mainly older folk. Harry Place was the senior minister and leader of the church. They had some young people with them and the youth pastor from Lliswerry, Gary Stirling, would become a great influence on me in the days to come. Gary was a Cardiff man who had once been a bit of a dropout, smoking pot and causing mayhem, till he found Christ in a remarkable way. He became an understudy to the Open Air Campaigners worker in the city, Pete Hodge, who would also play a prominent part in my own future development as a Christian. Looking back, it was a brilliant idea of Nancy's to suggest going to Lliswerry, where Gary and his wife, Gail, could take me under their wing and help me to become a fully committed follower of Jesus Christ.

So I joined the church that Sunday in my shirt and tie. By the evening service I had ditched the tie, as nobody else seemed bothered and I realized there was indeed no need for it.

In those early days of my newfound Christian faith I really was on fire for God. I just couldn't get enough of being at meetings and spending time with God's people. One Sunday after the morning service I asked Harry, "What have you got on around here midweek?"

He thought for a minute and then said, "Well, we've got Tuesday night's Bible study group, which is working through the Gospel of John, but I don't know if it would suit you because it mainly consists of a few elderly people going through the text page by page like they've been doing for years."

"Oh, well, that's fine then," I said. "I'll see you there!"

The next Tuesday evening I went along and just loved it. I revelled in being with people who knew and loved their Bible and could explain to me simply what it meant. Gary and others in leadership were just scratching their heads and asking each other, "What's going on here with this young guy?" because I turned up at everything. I was there for four months and they really looked after me. Those elderly Christians became my new family and I knew they really loved me. They were just the right people for me at that time. There were large and thriving evangelistic churches with plenty of young people just down the road from Lliswerry, which many might have presumed would be more suitable for this newly converted hard guy. God knew better, though, and placed me with the appropriate group of believers to help me in these infant stages of my discipleship.

When you think of how fussy some adoption agencies are about where they place their children, and how they vet and check prospective families before giving them children to adopt or foster, maybe it is no surprise that God takes such care about where he places those who are newly born again. Certainly, in my case, he could not have chosen better.

In Lliswerry I found people who would spend time with me and invite me into their homes. Practically every week some dear older person would invite me to their house for a meal. Considering my background and my record, there are many who might have criticized them for being naïve, but they were just what I needed as I tried to find my feet as a Christian. Each week I would head off to someone else's home, where we would share a traditional Sunday lunch of a lovely roast dinner and afterwards they would stick hymns on the stereo, and it was just wonderful. Even the aroma of those joints of lamb or beef roasting with onions was luxury for me after a worship service. They were amazing people and a terrific church, led by a great pastor and his wife. I owe a lot to the folk at Lliswerry Baptist Church and in particular to Harry and Alice, Gary and Gail.

In those early weeks following my encounter with the brass kettle and the voice of God I went through an Alpha course at the farm, run by Nancy and some of her friends. This was really helpful to me in laying down some good foundations for my faith. There were six of us on the course and we met once a week to eat together and then watch a video of the course founder, Nicky Gumbel from Holy Trinity Brompton in London (HTB), giving a talk. He covered subjects such as "Who is Jesus?", "Why did Jesus Die?", "How to Pray", "Does God Heal Today?", and many more besides. I found it fascinating and really helpful.

We had a "Holy Spirit day" for ourselves, and a dear old lady prayed for me to receive the Spirit. It was amazing. I was crying. Then somebody started laughing and we all went into absolute hysterics! From tears of conviction to tears of joy!

During these early days I also went on an Alpha course led by Troy Blankenship in Cardiff for the students of the university there. He wanted me to become part of the team running the courses, so as soon as the one in Cardiff was over I headed off to HTB with Troy to attend the annual Alpha conference. I not only loved the conference but found that the church at HTB seemed to be full of really positive people. On the second day I went out to pray during one of the breaks in what was once a cemetery near the church and is now a garden. I sat in the shade under a large old tree, watching other delegates together with families and office workers enjoying this patch of green in the middle of the concrete jungle that is central London.

Lifting up my heart in grateful prayer, I told God that if it was at all possible I'd love to work with these HTB guys one day. Two years later that prayer would be answered, but for the time being I returned to Wales full of the Holy Spirit, ready to help Troy run the student Alpha course in Cardiff.

I think it's fair to say that my first attempts at giving the talks were pretty disastrous. I became like a man possessed as I tried to convince these students of the existence of Jesus at the top of my voice! One of the guests told me I sounded like a typical Baptist preacher, and he didn't mean it as a compliment.

Nevertheless, I enjoyed running Alpha, and still do to this day. I believe that, in the right hands and if run properly, it is one of the most effective evangelistic resources we have in the church today. I continued to be involved in various forms of Alpha and loved it, not realizing that in the future I would be instrumental in leading large Alpha courses myself, in prisons, pubs, wine bars, churches, and barracks, through which I would see countless people come to their own faith in Christ.

"Alpha" is the first letter of the Greek alphabet and it means "beginnings". It certainly was for me.

25

"GOOD MORNING, GOD!"

After only a few months of this new Christian life I was on the mountain top as far as my emotions were concerned. I just loved God so passionately and wanted everybody around me to do so too. It must have been hard to live and work with me, but I was so much more enthusiastic about my new faith than I had been about my close protection work or my time in the army. I felt so loved and changed inside. I was swinging from the rafters, really, and would lay hands on and pray for anybody who had a problem or a pain around the farm and the building sites and gardens where I found work.

Guys used to get hacked off with me and tell me that I had gone crazy for God. Well, in some ways I had, but they didn't realize how far he had brought me and what this new start meant to me after all my struggles and failures. I was just loving Jesus and loving life.

But there was still one major area of concern and disappointment for me, and that was my relationship with Bev. She was thrilled to know I had got right with God, because by that stage she too had become a Christian and was attending a small Baptist church in the valleys. But we were divorced, and whenever I went over there to visit the children it was obvious that she did not want to spend time with me. I couldn't blame her after all I had put her through, but it hurt like a knife stuck deep in my heart.

Part of the problem was that I thought that now I was a Christian it should be automatic that Bev would love me and want to take me back. Bev said that she could see the transformation in me and knew that I was completely changed, but that there was no way she was going to get back with me. Looking back I realize how very badly I had treated her and the boys and can understand her hesitation, but at the time it was difficult for me to bear. I still loved Bev and wanted her to be with me in this new life that I was enjoying so much, but it just seemed that it was too much to expect.

I needed to learn that when God is at work he can do things in a remarkable way that is so much better than we could ever ask for or imagine, and that was what was about to happen to us.

Those first few months after my conversion in Wales were phenomenal. I felt so full of the Holy Spirit and in touch with God through the Bible and prayer, despite the sorrow and mystery surrounding my relationship with my ex-wife. I used to think that Jesus was just a figment of my parents' imaginations, but now I had met him and I loved him with all my heart. God let me enjoy him and his love then in a remarkable way. I used to go to sleep listening to hymns and I would wake up in the morning saying, "Good morning, God! What have you got for me to do today?" I was so in love with Jesus that it bubbled over into everything I did, and the fellowship at Lliswerry allowed me to be myself despite the occasional disruption that brought to their traditional way of doing things. For instance, they would normally sit to sing choruses, but I just couldn't sit down for sheer joy and excitement, so I would stand up and clap enthusiastically. As a result others in the congregation started standing too and in the end we were all on our feet, singing loudly and praising God with real fervour.

I think people began to feel that there was a bit of a breakthrough happening in the church. Harry was appreciative of this and we built up quite a friendship. He would spend time with me and try to answer my many questions and lead me deeper into God's ways.

One day Harry asked to see me and, once we were seated in his little office, or vestry, as he called it, he looked me in the eye and said, "Billy, I think you're definitely ready to be baptized. This seems to me to be one of those 'believe and be baptized' moments that you read about in the New Testament." Once he had explained that, in Bible days, people who became followers of Jesus were baptized by total immersion in water as a sign that their old life was gone and they had become new people by faith in him, I was convinced. Like many folk I had got confused and thought that baptism was only for babies, but now I could see that this was for me as a spiritual babe in Christ.

In order to prepare me for this great event Harry started coming out to the farm regularly so that we could do some baptismal classes together. He later told me that he felt that he had taken a tiger by the tail in these early days, as I was just bursting to start travelling around the Welsh valleys preaching Christ and proclaiming the good news of God's amazing love. We arranged that my service of baptism would be held on Easter Sunday in 2001. I was full of anticipation and energy but there was still one dark cloud in my sky. No matter how brightly the sun of my faith was shining, this one recurring shadow cast cold shivers down my spine: Bev didn't want to know me.

****

Two weeks before the date scheduled for my baptism, I was sitting at the farm feeling really upset. I had just come back from visiting Bev and the boys and had seen again how cool her behaviour was towards me. She wasn't hostile or nasty but she was guarded and restrained, making it clear that there was no mileage in our relationship. Back at the farm it was pouring with rain on a really dark night like the ones I remembered from exercises with the army up on the moors of Yorkshire. The wind was buffeting the windows and doors of the old house and the rain was pounding on the roof like an angry man trying to get my attention. Even the room itself smelt damp and it sounded as if there were rivers flowing in the gutters outside.

Suddenly I couldn't take it any more and, launching myself out of the old armchair, I stormed outside, slamming the door behind me. I stomped across the concrete farmyard with its slurry channels acting like river-beds for the rain and into the fields beyond, splashing through the puddles and ignoring the downpour. On and on I plunged, like a scene I recall from the film *Faith like Potatoes*,[9] where the main character, a Christian farmer in South Africa, rages against God in a heavy rainstorm out among his crops for taking the life of his little boy.

Just as with him, water was pouring down my face as rain mixed with tears and cascaded over my open mouth. I screamed out to God in a potent mixture of sorrow, rage, and longing. The heavy rain drenched me as I cried, as if the very

9   2006, directed by Regardt van den Bergh.

elements were mocking me in my distress. Soaked to the skin, I sobbed and pleaded with God. "O Lord, you know I want my wife back. I don't want anybody else, Lord, only her. You know how much I have hurt her and how right she is when she tells me about that. But, God, you have worked such a miracle in me – please change her mind!"

Just before I had gone outside I had come off the phone after trying without success to talk to Bev once again, and now as I stood in the rain I glanced down at my mobile phone and hurled it in frustration across the muddy field with an overarm action that might have won a test match in better conditions. It arced gracefully through the deluge and plopped into a far-off puddle, and I never saw it again, even though I searched for it the next day! Gradually my sobbing subsided and with it my distress, and I made my way back through the muck to the farmhouse, drenched and disheartened.

As I made my way in I met a minister who was leading one of the groups that was using the farm as a Christian retreat centre. He was sitting in an armchair beside the log fire in the main lounge and, as I squelched past him looking like Jonah, he looked up from his newspaper and asked softly, "Are you OK?"

"Not really," I replied with massive understatement, as I shivered in front of the blazing logs, trying desperately to get warm again.

He seemed genuinely concerned, so once my front had begun to thaw I turned round and squatted with my back to the fire to dry that side, and began to unburden my heart. The room filled with a scent like laundry drying on a clothes horse as I told him how much I regretted what I had done and how badly I had treated my family in the past. "But all that's changed now I've become a Christian," I insisted, "and I really know that I have become a different person now and I believe that I can be a good dad and husband again – though not in my own strength, of course, but with God's." I hardly paused for breath as I poured out all my sadness and despair about Bev's unwillingness to have me back and the distress I felt because the one thing I really wanted seemed now to be out of my reach for ever.

Calmly and lovingly he listened to me, nodding occasionally and asking me a few simple questions for clarification of my story. Then he opened his Bible and asked me to read out a verse. It was Matthew 6:33 and I read, "But seek first his kingdom and his righteousness, and all these things will be given to you as well." Then he looked at me with compassion and said, "I believe what God is saying to you, Billy, is that you must seek first the kingdom of God and his righteousness and then all these things will be given to you. I think that maybe you have put Bev in that first place and God is waiting for you to let her go before he can answer your prayers."

Suddenly I realized that he was right, and I was mortified by my own mistake. I had allowed my feelings for Bev to come before my love for Jesus and my trust in him and his plans for me. It was almost as if I had been addicted to Bev rather as I had to drugs and alcohol, depending on her instead of on God to meet my needs.

Once this became clear to me I just wanted to put it right straight away, so we bowed together in front of the fire and prayed. As we prayed I consciously let go of my desire for Bev and handed it over to God. I said, "Lord, I give up Bev to you and I seek your kingdom above everything else. I don't know if I'll ever get her back again but I choose to trust you. In the name of Jesus, amen."

Even as we sat up again I knew that something good had taken place inside me and that things were somehow different. I can't remember that minister's name, but I owe him a great debt. I felt that angels from God had been squatting alongside me beside the fire as we were praying. It felt as if something had definitely been cut, and despite the fact that I was still really sad I went upstairs and had a great night's sleep. I had prayed the prayer of relinquishment, which is so important if we want to know God and serve him with all our heart. The next day I woke up and said, "Good morning, God!" as usual, and went off to do my work with a new perspective on my circumstances. I really had let go of Bev and God knew that I had and was starting to work out his own plan and purposes in a way that was beyond my ability to achieve, and which would blow my mind!

We had invited my family to come down from Scotland to attend my baptism. My mum and dad travelled together with my sisters. Bev later told me that on the morning of the day of my baptism, Easter Sunday, she and my younger sister, Judith, shared a car on the way to the service at Lliswerry. As they drove, Judith asked Bev, "I hope you don't mind me asking, but do you feel there is any chance at all for you and Billy to be together again?"

"No, none at all," Bev replied quickly, "none whatsoever. I love him in a way, mind, but not how I used to do, and I wish him all the best. I really hope he makes it and all that, but no, there's no future for him and me." She then told Judith, "There's been too much that's gone on and there's no way we are going to get together again." She was defiantly maintaining her stand even though she was willing to come and see me get baptized. Of course I did not know that at the time; I was just so elated that they would all be there on this very special occasion.

26

MAKING A BIG SPLASH

When the time came for the evening service of baptism there was a great buzz of excitement in the air at Lliswerry Baptist Church. People were chatting loudly in their seats and I could hear Bev's confident voice above the others as they laughed at some shared joke or other. The fragrance of the many Easter flower arrangements filled the air, and because the water heater had been working for twenty-four hours or so the atmosphere was really humid, like being in a greenhouse at Kew Gardens. The musicians started playing and at just the right moment Harry stood to welcome us all to this very special occasion. There were three other candidates for baptism that night and we sat together in a nervous group in the front row like young ballerinas waiting to perform our first dance in front of an audience.

Soon we were all singing our hearts out about the grace and mercy of God and celebrating his name. I felt a great glowing joy in my soul and must have been beaming like a hundred-watt light bulb. Then it was my turn to share my testimony, and I was virtually swinging from the rafters as I told the gathered crowd everything from day one right the way through to that special moment. The only things I missed out were to do with the negative aspects of my childhood, which I suppose was out of respect for my dad and also because I don't think at that stage I fully appreciated the effect it had had on me. That would come later in my Christian experience.

I remember saying in a loud voice, "I was once lost but now I'm found – I was blind but now I can see", and the people cheered as I made my way towards Harry, who was standing in the baptistry. It comprised a tank sunk into the floor at the front of the church, about 4 metres long and maybe 2 wide, with steps down into it from one end. Usually covered by special carpeted floorboards, it was opened up with great enthusiasm on those all too rare occasions when someone wanted to be baptized.

The water was much warmer than I had expected, having been heated all night and throughout the day by an immersion heater. Down the steps I went, and waded in up to my waist alongside Harry. I waited anxiously for him to speak.

"Billy Gilvear, do you confess Jesus Christ as Lord of your life?" he demanded loudly.

"YES!" I shouted, and the congregation laughed.

"Do you renounce the devil and all his works?"

"I DO!" and again the building filled with the sound of rejoicing.

"Then, upon the confession of your faith, I baptize you in the name of the Father, the Son, and the Holy Spirit, amen."

At the sound of the word "amen" I held my breath, and Harry plunged me backwards under the water.

It was an amazing feeling. The old Billy Gilvear was dead. The punching, brawling, boasting would-be gangster with his alcoholism and drug addiction was buried right under those baptismal waters. For a moment they seemed to fill my nostrils and ears and I wondered if I would resurface at all, but the next I felt so clean and still, as if back in my mother's womb, that I would gladly have remained there. Then, with a shout and punching the air, I was up again, spluttering and splashing.

"Raised to new life in Christ" called Harry above the praises of the people in the church building and the sound of the band starting up. Then, as I stood dripping with the waters that represented hope and life to me, Harry laid his hands on my head and prayed for me. He asked God to fill me with his Holy Spirit and to use me in his work. Quoting Psalm 37 verse 4, he prayed that as I would delight myself in God and his service, so God would give me that which my heart most desired. What I could not have known then was that the same Holy Spirit was speaking to Bev, and that what he was saying to her would change my life for ever.

Much later, Bev told me that she was feeling quite apprehensive right up to the point when I told my story. She was moved by the testimony, and she saw something in me that night that she had never seen before. Apparently, when I said, "Once I was blind but now I can see", the Lord spoke to her and asked, "Bev, can't *you* see? You have been praying for a man in your life. Can't you see that this is the man?"

She wondered what God meant by that, but at that very moment the Holy Spirit spoke to her heart again so clearly that she was left in no uncertainty. He told her, "You can love this man again." She later explained to me that she was sure this was the voice of the Lord because it cut right across all the preconceptions that she had and all her instincts of self-preservation and for the protection of her children. When the meeting was over and I had changed into some dry clothes, she came up to me and gave me a hug of a kind that I hadn't had for a long time from her. In recent times there had always been something in her perfunctory hugs that seemed to be saying, "I feel for you after all you've been through", or even "I pity you". This time, though, I sensed genuine warmth, and for the first time in years my ex-wife looked into my eyes and smiled lovingly. The whole experience had really touched her and the Holy Spirit had spoken to her, though I did not know the full extent of it that evening.

The next day she phoned me and said, "Billy, I think God's told me I can love you again", and that was the beginning of a long but amazing journey for us both. We arranged to meet that day, and we started courting again. We had never really courted the first time round in the army, as military relationships were just not like that, so this time we did it properly. We went to the cinema together and started attending church and Christian events as a couple. We spent some quality time in each other's company in the beautiful South Wales countryside and by the sea. We walked and talked, laughed and prayed, played and just enjoyed discovering one another again.

It was wonderful. If I had been on cloud nine before this, I was way up in the stratosphere now. We spent a full year being like that together and working through some of our problems. We had a lot to unpack because of all the lying and deceiving that I had indulged in while we were married and also because of things that had happened to us while we had been apart. It was important for us to rebuild so much that had been completely broken down, but now we were not doing it on our own. God was working on our hearts and our relationship, and we were both growing in grace. We often reminded each other of God's promises, and one in particular that seemed very appropriate. It's found in the Old Testament book of Joel, where God says to his people, "So I will restore to you the years that the swarming locust has eaten" (Joel 2:25, NKJV). Our family life had been devastated by sin and deceit just like locusts swarming over crops in a field, and now God was gradually restoring to us so much of what we had lost.

But the process could not be hurried. Bev's family, in particular, were very unsure about us getting together again, and said so quite openly. I would have just rushed right on into getting married again, but there was no way Bev was going to countenance that at first.

27

"ON YOUR KNEES, PAL!"

One day in August 2001 Bev invited me over to see the boys and to stay for a meal, which she cooked for me. We laughed and cried together as we once again enjoyed the sheer wonder of how things had changed for us. I had a secret plan that day. I wanted to propose to her again, and had gone equipped with a ring hidden in my pocket. After the meal, when the boys were in bed, I got down on one knee and asked Bev if she would become my wife. This time I did things properly, except that I fumbled with the ring and tried to place it on the wrong finger. Wonder of wonders, she said yes, straight away. I was over the moon. We both wanted a relationship based on love, fun, trust, and friendship, whereas our first marriage had been built on lust and a desire to party.

It would be nearly a year before we would get married at Lliswerry Baptist Church, but there was so much to do to prepare for what was to be the wedding that we had never had. Our first wedding had been a mess, really, and no more than the collision of two lost souls, void of hope and faith. This one would be a celebration of love, faith, and the goodness of God.

As the service was to be at Lliswerry, Harry wanted to give us some marriage preparation beforehand. He reckoned that we needed it, and boy was he right! He and Alice invited us over to their house for the sessions, or, if Bev could not find a babysitter, they would come to Bev's place. They shared with us their own journey through marriage and ministry, and were very honest with us. We looked at issues such as the priority that we would need to give to real communication in our new marriage, and how to cope with conflict. This was certainly all fresh to me, as I had pretty much kept Bev in the dark throughout our earlier time together about what was really going on in my head and my life. Yet unless a husband and wife can truly communicate, the relationship will be very troubled and may well fail.

Harry spoke about the need to plan regular quality time together and showed us how we could work that into our weekly schedule and protect it as much as possible. Most helpfully of all, they modelled before us how a Christian couple should laugh, share, and pray together. They let us in on the inside track of their own relationship and it looked so different from the one we had known.

As we listened to them we began to look at each other in a new light. My love for Bev had always been strong, but now I was beginning to see her as much more of an equal partner in this relationship. Mutual respect was beginning to grow where previously we had walked over each other's emotions and often treated one another badly. We were being introduced to the Christian concept of marriage, which is so different from the many other models of long-term relationship that are around today. Bev wanted to repent of how she had treated me in the early days while she was still in the army and before our first cancelled wedding. I was full of remorse about how I had subjected her to so much abuse all along and had neglected her needs and desires almost entirely. Tears flowed fairly freely at those training sessions, especially towards the end.

The wedding itself, on 20 July 2002, was an incredible day. It was the marriage ceremony we should have had all along, and which God was now restoring to us. My friend Dave was my best man. He had been such a good mate to me throughout all my struggles, and he was overjoyed to be asked to come and be my right-hand man. He came up from the south coast of England with his wife and his mum. This Irish Catholic lady had played an important role in my wilderness years because she had taken me into her home when I had literally nowhere else to go. Then I had my family from Scotland, and some of them weren't committed Christians so they must have been really curious about what was going on. Jordan and Jack, my two fine sons, were resplendent in their tartan kilts, as was I, and acted like mini best men. I was so proud of them.

After the service, which saw the church packed to overflowing for the occasion, we all went back to the farm for a reception that had been laid on by our friends and fellow church members. This was a dream wedding on a shoestring, and it was truly fantastic. In preparation for the great day we had cleared out one of the big barns and stacked hay bales around the place so that people could use them as seats. At one end there was a stage for the band, draped with both the Scottish and the Welsh flags. For ten years afterwards a tattered remnant of that Scottish flag hung from the rafters in that working barn. On the day, the sweet fragrance of the hay combined with the heat of the sun and the sound of acoustic guitar music plus a harmonica to create an idyllic country-

and-western scene. There was plenty of chatter and laughter among the people and in the background the cattle were mooing and dogs barking out of curiosity – and with some degree of annoyance.

The local pub, from which I had once been banned because of my appalling behaviour, closed for the day and the owner and his wife came up to the farm to run the bar. Such was the transformation they had seen in me that they said it was something they really wanted to do. There in the barn we held a céilidh, a traditional Gaelic social gathering that usually involves folk music and dancing. One of the Christian guys I had met in Cardiff had a brother who was in a céilidh band, and he came with his team. Children threw themselves into the heart of the bouncy castles put up in the farmyard over which I had stomped in my anger at what I thought was Bev's final rejection of me as a husband. We danced and laughed and celebrated just a few hundred metres from the slurry tank in which I had been going to kill myself. In fact, I had dug out from its hiding place the rope that I had prepared as a noose, and this was on display for all to see like a trophy of war after a great victory has been won, as was Nancy's brass kettle, now resplendent in all its Brasso'd™ glory. There was a real village-carnival atmosphere filling the place where I had known such misery and where my life had once not seemed worth living.

On this momentous day God was being glorified even without anyone standing up on a soapbox to preach. The evidence of the grace and mercy of God, together with his redeeming power, was clear for all to see, and there were many non-Christians there to witness it. I didn't drink any alcohol that day and neither did my dad, but we were both up on that dance floor free of any inhibitions as we whooped and reeled in the heady atmosphere of celebration and praise.

The next day Bev and I set off for our honeymoon, leaving my mum and dad to stay on to look after Jordan and Jack. We went to Cephalonia, a very romantic Greek island where the novel and film *Captain Corelli's Mandolin* were set.[10] It was all that we might have imagined it to be: hot, peaceful, romantic, and fabulously beautiful. We met a couple of girls on the outward flight who were from another Baptist church in South Wales, and one of them was the daughter of one of the ministers there. At the airport he said to me, "Billy, while you're there will you just keep an eye on my daughter for me, please?" So there we were on honeymoon, plus keeping an eye out for these two girls! But we actually had great fellowship with them during the week, as well as plenty of quality time to ourselves.

Thinking back on those days, I could not have been happier if you had given me a million pounds! My favourite verse from the Bible is John 10:10: "Jesus said, 'I have come that they may have life, and have it to the full.'" This is a verse that I understood as a personal reality after my conversion and my remarriage to Bev. It was the absolute best time of my life, and I don't think I will ever experience anything like that again until I get to glory. Maybe God gave me a taste of heaven on earth because I had already had my fill of hell. At this time in my life I felt as if all those Bible stories were coming alive, like the one about the party that the loving father threw for his prodigal son when he returned, and how there will one day be a great wedding feast in heaven. All these marvellous things from God's word seemed to become very special to me

10   Novel by Louis de Bernières, 1994, and film by John Madden, 2001.

during the period from my conversion through my baptism followed by our dating, and to the wedding and beyond. It was just incredible.

28

WALKING THE WALK

Once we returned to South Wales I moved in with Bev and the boys and paid the bills by working as a landscape gardener with one of the guys from the farm. Gary Stirling, the youth pastor at Lliswerry, was involved at the time with Open Air Campaigners in Cardiff, and often went to the city to work alongside the full-time open-air missioner, Pete Hodge.

So excited was I with my newfound faith and by being at that stage newly married and minted that I was really desperate to be doing something for the Lord. Pete and Gary were kind to me and allowed me to shadow them and after a short time to start taking part in open-air evangelism myself, mainly in Queen Street, Cardiff and around the capital's centre. They taught me how to shape and craft my personal story, which they called my testimony, in a way that would be most effective in just a few minutes. They took me with them when they were leading assemblies at schools around Newport and Cardiff, and taught me how to use a sketchboard in the high street as a way of gathering a crowd and telling a gospel story. They told me that they felt God had called me to be an evangelist, which was a term I remembered from my childhood but had never fully understood. Now I know that they were right, and that spreading the good news about God's love is the main thing that turns my light on and brings joy to my heart.

Leading another person to Christ is the greatest privilege any man or woman can have in this world. The joy of sharing that moment with someone exceeds any reward on earth. As the Bible book of James tells us, "Remember this: whoever turns a sinner from the error of their way will save them from death and cover over a multitude of sins" (James 5:20). Pete would also take me round with him on a Sunday to some of the many different churches that supported his ministry. If he was going somewhere to preach he would get me to begin by sharing my testimony for five minutes or so before he delivered the main message. We might do that anywhere in South Wales, up in the valleys or in the main centres such as Swansea, Newport, or Cardiff, or even across the border in places like Gloucester, Worcester, Bristol, and others around the south-west of England. He would usually take notes while I was speaking, and on the long drive back home he would debrief me. It was always really helpful stuff and very constructive criticism, for which I was truly grateful. Throughout my army career I had been used to the concept of continual training and development with regular assessments and correction as part of that. It has always been a mystery to me since becoming a Christian how poor we are in the churches at both giving constructive feedback and receiving it. I welcomed it from Pete, and it served me well in those early days.

Soon, however, I was to discover that living the Christian life is not plain sailing, and that the worst of my troubles would come from other Christians. The kind of opposition and mockery we encountered on the streets did not bother me at all. I felt a bit like John the Baptist, who famously stood up in public calling both high and low to repent. When I took flak for doing that it seemed to be a fairly natural outcome, and in any case I had read in my New Testament that Jesus warned his followers that because the world had hated him it would hate them too. My army training had prepared me to deal with what was really just a form of unarmed combat – debating matters of faith with hostile unbelievers!

What I found more difficult to cope with were the misunderstanding and rejection that would come from others within the churches, especially once we had moved on from Lliswerry, where I had first been nurtured in Christ. In retrospect, I think that some of this opposition was the result of my own excessive enthusiasm and the fact that I challenged so much in church life that I did not understand or in which I could see no point. Yet, beyond that, there were definite moments when Satan, the accuser, tried to derail my faith. The actions of certain individuals, usually older men, struck an unhappy chord in my subconscious, like a clumsy soldier stamping on a deeply buried landmine left over from a previous conflict. The resulting explosions nearly destroyed my faith, but God is faithful and he taught me many lessons through those experiences and more, so that today I am still serving him and the gospel.

29

ENLISTING AGAIN FOR ACTIVE SERVICE

It was a warm and airless night in our house, which was unusual for South Wales. Bev and I had been out for a meal with friends that evening and my delicious steak was lying just a bit heavy on my stomach. I couldn't sleep, but it was for spiritual not digestive reasons. For a long time I tossed and wriggled in bed, hearing Bev's steady breathing and aware that if I didn't get up I would soon wake her. Raising the duvet carefully, I crept away to the tiny lounge/diner downstairs and turned on a sidelight.

I wanted to pray but found it difficult to do so because my mind was in turmoil. I began to worship the Lord, thanking him for all he had done in my life and also calling on him to reveal his path for me. As I was doing so a picture began to form in my mind. It was strangely clear to me, with its vivid colours, and I felt a bit as I imagine the apostle Peter must have felt in Acts chapter 10, when he was given the mental picture of a large blanket spread before him while he was praying. Peter saw animals in his vision but I saw soldiers in mine. There before me was the image of the very first church into which I had been led on Sunday parade as a rookie Junior Leader so many years before. It was quite a remarkable building in that the roof touched the ground on either side of the pews in a kind of A-frame, with steep sides lined underneath with pine. It seemed like a Scandinavian design that had somehow been transplanted into a British barracks.

Into my vision marched a whole formation of soldiers, pouring in through the central doors and taking their places in the pews. Then those huge wooden doors were slammed shut behind them, leaving me outside, like the scene at the State Opening of Parliament when Black Rod is excluded from the House of Commons. I stood there banging with my fists on the door, frantically trying to gain entrance.

Overwhelmingly, the emotion I felt was a burning desire to go inside and tell those soldiers in the chapel that Jesus is alive, but I couldn't get in. The way was barred to me, and I felt such sadness. Then I was given a scroll and, in an amazing way, once I had the scroll in my hands the great doors just opened up in front of me and I was allowed to enter. As I did so the eyes of every soldier were on me as I walked to the front of the building. Strangely, once there I noticed that there was no chaplain or padre at the front, so I turned to address the military audience and was able to talk to them and share my testimony.

Around the same time as I had my night vision, Harry had been woken in the middle of the night with a real burden to pray for me. As he did so he felt led by God to some words of the prophet Micah in the Bible, which say, "He will stand and shepherd his flock in the strength of the Lord, in the majesty of the name of the Lord his God" (Micah 5:4).

When Harry shared that verse with me I sensed that it was very significant and wrote it down inside my Bible, where I still have it to this day. As we discussed my recent night-time vision and the possible relevance of this verse for me, Harry said, "Billy, I think God's calling you into some sort of ministry and for that you are going to need some kind of formal training." Following that, one or two other people also came up to me and encouraged me to pursue training for ministry, and I became convinced that this was God trying to get through to me. Maybe that training would give me the scroll from my vision and open doors of opportunity for me to share my story with others.

In the light of my military background and the picture that had come to me in the night, I really wanted to become an army chaplain. That did not turn out to be God's plan for me, but the vision was fulfilled in many powerful ways. I have visited army units and regiments at home and overseas on many occasions, sharing my faith and my testimony with soldiers and officers alike. Often I went as part of the Alpha for Forces initiative, an offshoot of the Alpha Course, based at HTB in London. At other times I went at the invitation of army chaplains or Christian officers who wanted their personnel to hear my story. I even visited the chapel in my vision again, as God brought me opportunities to tell the good news of his love for men and women in uniform.

Not knowing any of this at that early stage, however, I realized that if I were going to become a chaplain to the forces it would mean doing some kind of training, but I also thought that to be a "padre", as we called them, I would have to become an Anglican vicar. I know now that this is not the case. In fact in 2011 the army's newly appointed chaplain general was a Baptist! Of course they do have to have been ordained by a recognized church denomination, but I remembered that chaplains always seemed to be Anglicans or Roman Catholics. As I knew that I was not a Catholic, I rang the Anglican Church in Wales to enquire how I could go about getting ordained. The response was quite cool really, though not that surprising when you think about it, with this brash young Scotsman phoning up out of the blue. I was then advised that maybe the Anglican college at Oak Hill would be more up my street theologically, so I phoned them. They were very warm and invited me to London to meet them for a preliminary chat. Meanwhile Harry was always in the background, praying for me and watching out for my welfare, and he said, "Well look, Billy, you are a member of a Baptist church, so have you considered Spurgeon's College?"

I knew that it was an evangelical training college for Christians entering ministry, mainly within the Baptist Union but also beyond, so, because of Harry's recommendation, together with the fact that he had trained there, I made some enquiries and Bev and I went to see it. I really loved what I saw and met Peter Stevenson and Nigel Wright, who was then the principal, and they said it would be great if I would apply and join. So, in an amazing turnaround, that September, the boasting brawler, bodyguard to the stars, divorced and then remarried, ruined and rescued again, little Billy Gilvear, entered Bible college as a part-time student. In many ways it was very hard being there, and I felt tremendously inadequate for the task, but with my Bible open in front of me and the prayers of so many wonderfully supportive friends surrounding me, I began the serious business, as the army would have put it, of preparing for active service.

✳✳✳✳

As part of my studies during that first year at Spurgeon's I needed to be more closely linked to the leadership of a Baptist church. My evangelism soon brought me to the attention of the leaders of a big city church, and I found myself working with their young people and pretty much joining their staff. If all had gone well I would have become the student pastor, with responsibility for their branch church in a nearby small town, as well as continuing my studies, but it was not long before somebody in the eldership trod on a landmine that was still buried in my heart. He lied about me, betraying my trust, and when called to account for my alleged misdemeanour before the entire eldership, I felt that I had no alternative but to humble myself and apologize without trying to defend my position. After all, who would believe the word of this recently converted ex-drug addict against that of a trusted elder of the church, even if I was a Bible student now?

Afterwards I went out and wept bitterly, telling Bev that if this was how Christians behaved I was not sure I wanted anything to do with them.

And so began a long road of discipleship and service that has included many disappointments, which have forced me to face up to the bewilderment I have felt when Christian leaders, who often became father figures to me, have acted in ways that have hurt me or my family. For quite some time I struggled through this particular period of disillusionment, finding excuses for not being in church, such as taking my son Jordan to rugby practice on Sunday mornings, as he was turning out to be a really good young player. I withdrew from the Spurgeon's course at that juncture but they refused to give up on me, urging me to find a way back. Bev was patient and persistent with me, though, and many of our Christian friends understood what I was going through and continued to support and encourage us.

Then the college got in touch and told us that there was a church in Gillingham in Kent that was willing to take me on as an assistant student pastor, working under the oversight of David and Allison John, who were leading the church. If I accepted their offer I would be welcome to resume my course at Bible college and also a house would be provided for my family. I was reluctant at first. I felt such a failure, as so often before and even since. Yet Bev was steadfast, convinced that this offer was from God, and in my heart of hearts I knew that she was right. So we crossed the Severn Bridge once again and headed for London and nearby Gillingham, where a whole new adventure was about to begin.

****

I was pleasantly surprised by how our lives began to change for the better once we returned to the path of study and Christian service that God had clearly set out for us. At the same time, I also found myself back in jail! While living and working in Gillingham I became the Free Church Chaplain for the Rochester Young Offenders Institution (RYOI), thanks to the team at HTB. By this stage I had been given the opportunity to share my testimony at various Alpha launch nights, particularly with Alpha for Forces and Prisons, and thus began my working relationship and friendship with some of the team from HTB, particularly Paul Cowley, Emmy Wilson, Tim Sait, and Jerry Fields.

On one such occasion, after I had spoken, Tim asked if I would share my testimony at the Alpha course launch night in RYOI. As I lived only a couple of miles away, this was really convenient. After my talk there, as Tim was rounding things up, the senior chaplain asked me if I would consider helping to run the course with the team that was already there. I agreed, and the following week I turned up to help – but was shocked to discover that I was actually required to run it!

By the end of the course I had struck up such great relationships with staff and prisoners alike that I was asked to stay on as Free Church chaplain. I loved working in RYOI because I learned a lot about myself through my experiences there. I could see myself so clearly in many of these young offenders, and realized how much God had done for me in bringing me into this new life in Christ. I felt that I really understood them, and they appeared to respond warmly to that fact.

In addition to my roles as prison chaplain and student minister, I also went to various military establishments in both the UK and Germany with the Alpha for Forces team, sharing my testimony and running Alpha training days for military chaplains. It was an exciting time and I really do thank God for the folk from HTB and the opportunities they have given me as well as the love they have shown me. In the decade that followed, thanks to Alpha for Forces and Prisons, I travelled the world training and sharing my testimony as well as delivering Alpha talks in countries such as Nigeria and South Africa. I have also preached on my own mission trips in Pakistan, India (with BMS, formerly the Baptist Missionary Society), the USA, and all over Europe. In time I became an associate evangelist of the Philo Trust led by J. John, who has also gone on to be a real encouragement to me. The relationship with him has been a particular help and has enabled me to network with some key names in the world of evangelism.

30

THE GREAT QUESTIONS OF LIFE

I guess for me the big question throughout my life has always been, "Who am I?" It's a really big question and I know that I'm not alone in asking it, but it has always been a concern for me. I've rattled that question around in my head for as long as I can remember. I don't know if you've ever done that, or are even doing it now at this stage in your life, but I feel that over the years I have found at least some answers to my search. I know now that God is real, that he is made of love, and that he has got a good plan for my life. As you know, I have not always been aware of that and have certainly not always lived it out, but in my heart of hearts I acknowledge the fact. God has said, "Before I formed you in the womb, Billy" (and I guess you could put your own name there too), "I knew you, before you were born I set you apart…", and "'For I know the plans I have for you,' declares the Lord, 'plans to prosper you and not to harm you, plans to give you hope and a future.'"[11]

That's God's "Plan A" for our lives, and that plan stands regardless of what we do. God knew me while I was still in my mother's womb and he watched over my formation, making

11 Jeremiah 1:5 and 29:11.

sure that I was born safely into this world. At my service of infant dedication in the Congo there was a witch doctor nearby who hated my parents and their work and who cursed them and their newborn child. But not even Satan can stop God from loving us, and God waited patiently over decades for me to come to my senses and respond to him. So I entered the world in the middle of a struggle for survival, and as I grew up and became the tragic, rebellious Billy that you have read about in this book I sometimes almost lost that battle because of my attempts at suicide and my destructive lifestyle choices.

But this entrance into the world and this struggle in my early life with a Christian father who, because of his own unmet needs, did some horrible things to me made me very confused. I didn't know who I was. My self-esteem and my sense of self-worth had been punched out of me, and what I learned very early on was that to survive in this world without being tortured like that again I really had only two options. I could either retreat into a fantasy world disengaged from reality, or I could wear a mask.

I soon found that by putting on certain masks at certain times I could please people and would hear the magic words "Well done, Billy, good job", and that had such an impact on my life because I had never heard them from my father. So I went through life trying to please people, whatever it took and whatever mask I had to wear to achieve it. This was because I wanted people to like me and I didn't want to be hurt any more. The army gave me an identity, but it wasn't the real me. Although I had a successful army career during which I met Bev, who became my wife, and everything seemed right and well with the world, it still wasn't me inside. I knew it wasn't what God had designed me for. His plan was for loving fellowship with him through Jesus Christ, and the service of others in his name. Despite having a reasonably successful military career I was still feeling empty inside. I had no real passion for what I was doing, other than to succeed and impress others.

I often feel that one of the signs that someone is really fulfilled in their God-given pattern is that they have energy and passion. Throughout most of my time in the army and beyond I was devoid of passion, and my energy was largely fuelled by anger and the desire to please others. This endless searching and trying to please people meant that I remained very insecure, even in my relationship with Bev, because I feared that she would leave me. I had this deep-seated fear that I would be abandoned and rejected, and it followed me through my childhood and on into the army and my time in London. Eventually my own behaviour, driven by that fear of rejection, was the very thing that caused others to reject me, including Bev. But God's Plan A was always there in the background, just waiting for me to come round.

My search for the answer to that question of identity took me into the hedonistic world of celebrity culture and the closely allied arena of drugs, drink, and promiscuity. There I discovered that even famous people who seemed to have everything that I could want were, in fact, wearing masks too. Their pockets and bank accounts may have been full but on the whole their hearts were troubled and empty. Becoming like them in conduct if not in riches, I sank into the grim underworld of crime that lurks behind the supply of drugs and the demands of a broken subculture. Of course the answer to my quest was not in these places. It was only once my masks of ego and arrogance were exposed for what they were, totally empty and meaningless before almighty God, that I heard his gracious voice telling me of a better way, and a different drum to which I could march if I so chose. And you can make that choice today too. Whatever masks you may be wearing to try to answer those inner questions or avoid the pain that you have come to fear, God still has a Plan A for your life and is waiting for you to choose it.

Receiving Christ as saviour and enlisting in his great cause was not the end of my struggle, though the pattern changed. In times of stress, when the temptation to drink and despise myself rose up again, I would come to see that now I have to fight these things in the strength that God gives, and not in my own. The apostle Paul said, "When I am weak, then I am strong" (2 Corinthians 12:10), not "When I am strong, then I am strong."

I have had to learn to depend on God's strength alone. There were times at Spurgeon's when I wanted to give up. It took me five years of study to complete what I should have done in two, but, hey – welcome to my world! I hit the wall halfway through and my principal, Nigel Wright, called me in to see him. I expected to be expelled or at least rebuked very severely, but instead he shocked me.

"Billy, I'm not giving up on you," he told me. "We can be here all day if you like and you can keep going round and round the same old mountain but I'm still going to be here and we're still going to love you. What's more, we're going to get you through this course because God has called you." In some ways I was almost hoping that he would say, "Right, we've given up on you – get out!"

In my previous life I had grown accustomed to expecting people to say, "You're no good. You're rubbish – just a good for nothing, and it's all your fault", because those were the kind of words I had so often heard, but through Christ I had entered a different world. Instead of rejection I received counsel, understanding, patience, and support until I graduated from the course. What a fantastic experience we had towards the end of our time at Spurgeon's and in Gillingham.

When we moved to Guernsey to join the full-time staff of a Baptist church we were all really excited, though I felt quite apprehensive. The island is one of the Channel Islands and lies about a hundred miles (160 km) south of the UK and just 25 miles (40 km) or so from the French coast. It is a self-governing crown dependency and has its own quaint laws and culture. The population is around 65,000 and it is an ideal place to bring up children.

My passion has always been evangelism, and initially I was appointed to be an evangelist on a team with two other pastors. Within a short time the health of one of them deteriorated rapidly and he had to stand down from active ministry, and after a year the other one retired. The process of finding replacements took the whole of the rest of our five years on the island, so I found myself as the part-time senior chaplain in the prison as well as looking after a congregation of 250 or so people. My passion for the prison role was electric. I really cared for the inmates and their families, and got close to several of the staff.

But the strain of also being the pastor of a busy church started to get to me. When two prisoners committed suicide in rapid succession I found myself sinking under the pressures of grief, high expectations, and self-destructive thoughts. I began listening to the devil's lies instead of filling my mind with God's truth. Part of my role had been to take the families of the dead prisoners into the mortuary to identify their bodies, and when

I saw the rope-burn marks on the necks of those dead young men I felt the devil mocking me because I had failed in my own suicide attempts. My thinking had become really skewed again and I was in trouble.

I resigned from the prison chaplaincy, with a heavy sense of regret. This was a difficult time and Bev was an absolute brick for me and the family, now expanded to include our other two children, Ben and Lydia. Of course I hurt them and people in the church, especially as the island is a small community where it is like living in a goldfish bowl with everyone watching every move you make.

I also found, however, a core group of people who believed God had a plan for me and who hung in there with me and my family until Jesus brought me back to square one again.

****

And that's where we all need to come and stay, at the point where we are ready to say, "God, I can't do this thing called life without your help and power." I have found over and over again that God's passion and his love are greater than my greatest need, and his Plan A still stands. Where others might have fallen and turned away I've fallen and turned back again to my Father in heaven, who knew me before I was born and who still has that amazing plan for my life. He made it possible through the one person that I'm really passionate about in life, Jesus. I'm in his army and he is my real celebrity hero, and I recommend him wherever I go. I have come storming home, not to any earthly place or address, but to a love that will not let me go.

If you want to ask Jesus to enter your heart, as I did, then you might find the following prayer helpful:

> Lord Jesus,
> I turn to you now, believing you are a God who changes lives.
> Please help me.
> I'm sorry for my selfish ways and the mess I'm in, but I believe now that your death meant life for me.
> I ask you to touch my life, forgive me, and change me for ever.
> Thank you, Jesus.
> Amen.

If you have prayed this prayer, then you should tell someone what you have done – your husband or wife, your girlfriend or boyfriend, your best mate, your parents – it doesn't matter. Just share with them the step you have taken, and why you have taken it.

Next, you are going to need support. Find a group of Christians (search online for a local church, if need be) and tell them what you have done.

I would be really pleased to hear from you. Write and tell me your story. You can reach me at storminghome@gmail.com

Billy

If you would like Billy to come and tell his story at an event, church service, dinner, army barracks, or prison, please contact him at storminghome@gmail.com